D0812088

CHRONICLES OF THE
CELTS

CHRONICLES OF THE

CELTS

IAIN
ZACZEK

COLLINS & BROWN

First published in Great Britain in 1996
by Collins & Brown Limited
London House
Great Eastern Wharf
Parkgate Road
London SW11 4NQ

Copyright © Collins & Brown Limited 1996
Text copyright © Iain Zaczek 1996

All rights reserved. No part of this publication may be reproduced, stored in a retrieval system, or transmitted, in any form or by any means, electronic, mechanical, photocopying, recording or otherwise, without the prior written permission of the copyright owner.

1 3 5 7 9 8 6 4 2

British Library Cataloguing-in-Publication Data:
A catalogue record for this book is available from the British Library

ISBN 1 85585 407 4

Editor: Liz Dean
Designer: Alison Lee
Picture Research: Katie Bent, Philippa Lewis

Original design: David Fordham
Illustrator: A R Jewell

Colour reproduction: HBM, Singapore
Printed and bound in Great Britain by Jarrolds

CONTENTS

INTRODUCTION

THE WORD 'CELTIC' CONJURES up many things. To some people, it evokes a hypnotic design from the *Book of Kells* or the Tara Brooch; to others, it is a plaintive song, accompanied by a lone fiddler or piper; or again, it is a mystical past, peopled with Arthurian knights and druids. All these notions have some basis in reality, but most are half-truths, seen through a veil of Romanticism. These, in turn, have been woven into the fabric of the Celtic tradition, which has captured the imagination of successive generations.

The true origins of the Celts lie deep in the mists of prehistory. They were a loosely-knit group of tribes, with connective elements of a common culture and a common language. Traces of these date back to the final stages of the Hallstatt culture (c. 700–500 BC), which was based in the area around Upper Austria and Bavaria. By the sixth century BC, Greek authors wrote of a people called the 'keltoi' in southern France and, a century later, Herodotus located them in the region around the Danube. In time, their settlements stretched from Turkey and the Balkans right across to western Europe. At the peak of their power, they were strong enough to sack both Rome (386 BC) and Delphi (279 BC). The memory of these victories was soon eclipsed, however, by the rise of the Roman Empire. Here, the lack of cohesion between the various Celtic tribes proved fatal. One by one, they were overrun or expelled from their territories. Eventually, they were pushed back to the western fringes of the continent.

The heyday of the ancient Celts coincided with the La Tène era, which flourished in the last centuries before Christ (c. 480–50 BC). During this lengthy period, their craftsmen developed a highly distinctive style of decoration. This consisted of a range of curvilinear motifs – such as spirals, interlacing and highly-stylized figurative forms – woven together to form intricate, maze-like patterns. Initially, these designs were applied to various forms of metalwork, the medium in which the early Celts excelled. However, their near-abstract quality made them extremely versatile, enabling the visual style of the Celts to survive long after they had waned as a political force. Christian artists, for example, could use the same patterns on the page of a manuscript or in the design of a chalice, without having any qualms about their pagan source.

This facet of Celtic culture has enjoyed great longevity. Many original artefacts have survived and their designs have been widely adapted and reused, right up to the present day. Indeed, it is this aspect of the Celts which is probably most familiar to people today. But, even though this is a fine tribute to the high quality of early Celtic craftsmanship, it tells us very little about the society that produced it. The Celts themselves left virtually no written records, and so we are largely dependent on their enemies – classical and Christian authors – for information about them.

These sources suggest that the Celts were a fierce, warlike people, who entered the battlefield with little fear of death; that they were ostentatious, loving gold and fine jewellery; and that they enjoyed feasting, boasting and eloquent speech. Not surprisingly, perhaps, the same sources also tended to dwell on some of their more lurid customs. Diodorus Siculus, for example, wrote about the practice of head-hunting, while Pliny and Strabo gave details of the druids' human sacrifices.

In addition to these contemporary accounts, we also have the evidence of the many Celtic stories and legends that have come down to us. Clearly, these are not as biased as the classical accounts, but they still have to be approached with a degree of caution because of the comparatively late date of the surviving manuscripts. Originally, the stories were transmitted orally over a period of centuries, before being written down. Philological evidence suggests that this transcription process may date from the seventh century, but existing versions of the major texts go back no further than the eleventh century.

The first storytellers

The Irish stories are the oldest. They predate the arrival of the first Christian missionaries, offering a unique insight into living conditions in Iron Age Europe. In the first place, they were memorized by a class of poets known as the filidh. Their training was very long and arduous – an early Irish document suggests that it lasted twelve years – and their repertoire was huge. In one early manuscript, for example, we are told that a fili named Forgall recited a different story to Mongán, a sixth-century king of Ulster, on every night between Samhain and Beltane. Further confirmation can be found in the Book of Leinster, which includes a list of the tales that a fili was expected to know. These amounted to around two hundred and fifty primscéla (main stories) and one hundred fóscéla (secondary tales).

It seems likely that the fili approached this mammoth task by learning the bare bones of the narrative and then extemporizing the details. This would explain why the surviving versions are so consistent in their general outline, but vary so much in their details. The oral method of transmitting stories is also reflected in the structure of some sections of the Táin. Often, there are unwieldy descriptive passages, where the storyteller warms to his task of discussing the rich array of armour and jewellery worn by his characters. Following these sections, however, the narrative can sometimes tail off disappointingly, as the speaker begins to grow tired.

The background to the Irish tales is of greatest interest to historians, as it appears to offer the clearest picture of the ancient Celts. Most Celtic territories eventually came under the Roman yoke, but Ireland never formed part of the Empire. As a result, the craftsmanship, the customs and the oral traditions of the old La Tène period were still flourishing when the first Christian missionaries arrived. It was only with the coming of the Vikings that the Celtic way of life finally changed.

Celtic values

The picture that emerges from the story of the Táin is of a society where courage, strength and fighting skill were all-important. These values were upheld by an aristocratic warrior class, which devoted most of its time to martial pursuits, and relaxed by playing hurley or fidchell. This class structure was bound together by an elaborate system of fosterage, wherein noble sons were often placed with neighbouring families until they reached adulthood. The system created strong bonds of loyalty within the various Celtic tribes, and was designed to offset some of the problems that arose from the lack of a centralized administration. This explains why, in the episode concerning Cú Chulainn's birth (see 'The Táin', page 22), so many Ulstermen offer to rear the child. It also accounts for the substantial number of foster-brothers and foster-fathers that crop up later in the narrative.

The cult of the hero

Nevertheless, this bonding process was completely overshadowed by the hero-cult in the early sagas. For, despite the overwhelming emphasis on warfare, strategy and teamwork are virtually non-existent in the *Táin*. Almost all the crucial victories are gained through individual acts of heroism. This is less evident in the adventures of the Fionn Cycle (see page 76), where the exploits are shared more evenly between a greater cast of characters. Here too, the background to the cycle is based upon a historical reality. Several genuine fianna (literally 'bands of warriors') are thought to have existed. Aedán mac Gabráin, for example, is said to have sent one such troop to Britain in 603, to aid his Pictish allies. The stories in the Fionn Cycle also reflect a gradual transition from epic to romance, and many commentators have seen Finn and his men as the prototypes for King Arthur and the knights of Camelot.

Both sets of tales provide useful insights into contemporary methods of warfare. In the *Táin*, for example, most of the leading figures fight in chariots, a skill that had long been associated with the ancient Celts. Archaeologists have unearthed sumptuous chariot-graves from the earliest La Tène period, showing how much attention was lavished on these war machines. Chariots were still in use centuries later, when Caesar came to write about his campaigns in Gaul. In his account, he described how the Celts used to drive into the fray at high speed, trying to instil fear into their opponents by shouting loudly and beating their weapons against the sides of their chariots. At this stage, the warrior would hurl his javelins, before descending to fight on foot. The charioteer, meanwhile, would retire to the fringes of the battle, ready to rescue his lord if the conflict should go against him. This life-saving function explains the close bond that is evident between warrior and charioteer in stories in the *Táin*, where the latter appears to act as a kind of confidant.

Cú Chulainn's prowess (see 'The Táin', page 42), also depended on a number of other factors. Firstly, there were his magnificent weapons, epitomized by his sword – the quasi-magical Gae Bolga. The Celts took particular pride in their arms, often giving them names and attributing specific personalities to them. They were also respectful of the craftsmen who made these splendid objects. The smith was treated with great honour in the Celtic world. He was granted special burial rites and enjoyed greater freedom to move from tribe to tribe. The Irish also revered a triad of craft-gods, headed by Goibhniu, the divine smith who forged weapons that never missed their mark.

Mystic warriors

The mystical importance attached to fine weaponry was only one of the many superstitions surrounding Celtic warfare. Classical sources detail the gaesatae, a special breed of warriors who wore only a torc when going into battle, believing that their nakedness would provide some form of supernatural protection. They also remarked upon the fierce screams and taunts made by Celtic fighters, and the way that they set upon their enemies in a manic frenzy. The importance of this last feature, so reminiscent of the savage, Norse berserkers, is clearly emphasized in the *Táin*. In a number of passages, Cú Chulainn works himself up into a terrible fury before going out to fight, undergoing a series of strange, bodily transformations in the process. Some of the shouting, referred to in classical texts, would probably have taken the form of boasts or challenges. The fulfilment of a boast was a matter of honour among Celtic warriors, and the narrator of the story was openly scornful of figures like Etarcomol, who failed to live up to their words.

The role of the challenge was more complex. Cú Chulainn issued a number of these in the *Táin*, frequently forbidding his enemies to pass beyond a certain point until they had performed some specified feat of strength. In doing this, he was laying a 'geis' upon the Connacht army. This geis (pl. gesa or gessa) was a form of taboo, preventing the recipient from undertaking certain types of action. It was taken very seriously, and any breach of it could result in the transgressor being ostracized by his tribe or even put to death.

The geis was used in a variety of ways in the early Irish epics. In many cases, it resembled a type of curse or enchantment. Thus Gráinne, in the tale of her elopement with Diarmaid (see 'Diarmaid and Gráinne', page 77), places a geis on her reluctant lover, which forces him to carry her away. Here, the power of the enchantment is so strong that it overrides laws of kinship, fealty and hospitality. Echoes of this type of taboo can still be seen in some of the Welsh tales. The entire plot of Culhwch and Olwen (see 'How Culhwch Won Olwen', page 91), revolves around a very similar kind of curse, invoked at the start of the story by Kilydd's new queen. Other gesa seem more trivial. One of Diarmaid's unsuccessful attempts to escape his dilemma involved the excuse that he was under a geis, which prevented him from leaving any royal residence through a wicket-gate. Not surprisingly, the resourceful Gráinne soon found a way to overcome this minor problem.

Not all gesa were restricted to a particular time or place. Cú Chulainn, for example, was under a geis not to eat dog-flesh. Similarly, Diarmaid was prohibited from hunting boars, while Conaire was barred from killing birds. The last of these taboos was related in *The Destruction of Da Derga's Hostel*, from the Ulster Cycle, when it transpired that Conaire's father had himself been a bird. Needless to say, each of these characters eventually broke their geis, and the dire consequences of committing such a terrible act provided a fertile source of inspiration for many storytellers.

Forbidden words

The original purpose of the Celtic gesa is unclear. The fact that so many of them relate to animals suggests that there may have been some association with a totem cult. Another theory is that they developed out of ancient druidic laws. Some of these remained in force for centuries, surviving well into the Christian era. The most common examples relate to forbidden words. Certain things could only be named by initiates, while outsiders were obliged to use a euphemism. Thus, in Ireland, it was standard practice to refer to the moon by the word 'gealach' (brightness), rather than by its more literal name. Similarly, in the Isle of Man, fishermen would never mention the moon directly while they were at sea, describing it instead as 'ben-reine ny hoie' (queen of the night). This superstition persisted until the nineteenth century.

Triple symbolism

Another ritual element that comes across in the sagas is the Celtic interest in number symbolism. In common with other peoples of the period, the Celts regarded the number three as sacred. Several of their deities took the form of a trinity, most notably the three craft-gods, the Morrigán (see page 50) and Brigid (see page 30). Significantly, devotees of the latter used to make offerings to her at the meeting point of three waters. Also, early cult images often had triple aspects – such as a head with three faces or a bull with three horns – and the triad was a traditional literary form, employed by both the bards and the druids. On a more basic level, this explains why so many numbers in the texts are expressed in batches of three – thrice twenty, thrice fifty, for example.

The Celts were equally interested in dualism. Evidence for this can be found throughout the various Celtic territories, even in the earliest periods. Many of the pillar-stones made in ancient Gaul, for instance, were topped with fierce-looking Janus heads. Comparable tendencies can be found in the literature, especially in Welsh and Breton sources. One of the most poetic examples occurs in the story of Peredur, when the hero visits the court of the King of Suffering (see 'Peredur, Son of Evrawc', page 122). Here, his adventures lead him into a strange valley, where he finds a tree that is half in bloom and half in flames. Similarly, in the Breton district of Loc-Envel, there is a large forest split into two sections. These are known as the Coat-an-Noz (Forest of the Night) and the Coat-an-Hay (Forest of the Day). Accordingly, it transpires, the local saint took the form of two twin brothers, who lived apart, each in their separate half of the forest.

These ritual overtones are relevant because, in spite of the accuracy of many historical details, the substance of the early Celtic stories remains essentially mythical. Humans mingle with gods, and the exploits of mortals are coloured by supernatural influences. Cú Chulainn is the son of a god and has magical weapons at his disposal. He clashes with men, but also with deities like the Morrigán. Medb, his principal adversary, is part-queen and part-divinity. She is sometimes described as a goddess of sovereignty and war, and she has the power to shape-shift and to bring about similar transformations in others.

These mythical elements are complicated by the fact that, unlike their classical counterparts, these deities are no longer blessed with awesome powers. The Morrigán, for all her fearsome reputation, can still be wounded and has to be healed by Cú Chulainn. He, in turn, requires similar help from Lugh, his father. In the Welsh tales, this divine weakness is more apparent. Pwyll, for example, is called upon to fight in the place of an Otherworld lord, the king of Annwn (see 'Pwyll Encounters Rhiannon', page 104). Quite literally, the gods have become shadows of themselves.

The action at the heart of the Ulster Cycle is also rooted in legend and ritual. Cattle thefts and raiding parties must have been a normal part of everyday life in the La Tène period, but it is always plain that this conflict is far from ordinary. The bulls that are the source of the original dispute are not real animals, but shape-shifting magicians. As such, they can probably be associated with the bull cults, which were common to many of the Celtic peoples. Among other things, the bull symbolized wealth, strength and fertility. Cult images of bulls have been found in Hallstatt graves, dating back as far as the seventh century BC. There is also considerable evidence that bulls were

sacrificed. Pliny described a particular festival, when the druids sacrificed two white bulls. This rite was timed to coincide with the appearance of the horned or crescent moon. Several of the scenes depicted on the Gundestrup Cauldron also relate to the sacrifice of these animals.

For the Irish, the bull was intimately connected with the sacred kings of Tara. Their selection involved a ceremony called a Tarbhfhess. In this, a bull was ritually slaughtered by druids. Its meat and the broth in which it was cooked were then given to a selected individual. Next, the man was put to sleep and an incantation of truth was chanted over him by the druids. This was meant to send him into a dream, in which he would see a vision of the new high king. If the sleeper tried to conceal the content of his dream or lied about it, then, so the legend went, the gods would condemn him to a painful death.

The bull cult was deeply embedded in Celtic culture and some elements were later adapted by Christian missionaries. It seems likely, for example, that the quasi-mythical figure of St Cornély, the patron saint of Carnac, took over some of the functions of an ancient bull-priest. He is revered as the protector of horned beasts and on 13 September, the date of his Pardon, there is a public benediction of the cattle in the region. Nineteenth-century commentators also mention another semi-pagan custom. Whenever cattle in the district were sick, they were brought in silence to the front of the church and then taken beyond it to St Cornély's fountain. There, water was poured over them, before they were returned to their respective farms. Evidence for the original bull cult is confirmed by the existence of numerous carvings of horns on some of Carnac's dolmens, and by the discovery of a bronze statuette of a bull at a nearby Gallo-Roman villa.

Authorities on Celtic material tend to focus particular attention on the early Irish texts, because they are far less 'contaminated' than the literatures of other Celtic areas. Our oldest versions of the stories from Wales and Brittany, for example, are thought to date back to the eleventh and twelfth centuries respectively, even though they reflect traditions that are considerably older. Nevertheless, because of the longer gap in their transmission, the Celtic sources have been distorted somewhat by Christian, French and English influences.

In spite of this, it is intriguing to see how some Celtic elements were passed from one region to the next, undergoing subtle transformations in the process. The strand of equine imagery in the stories in this volume provides a case in point. There is no doubt that the horse was greatly revered in the Celtic world, both as a symbol of high status and for its usefulness in times of war. As a result, horses were employed in a variety of funerary rites and in certain types of sacrifice. Indeed, the fact that such a costly animal was ever sacrificed is a measure of its sanctity in some areas.

In the Ulster Cycle, there are two important episodes involving horses. The first of these relates to the birth of Cú Chulainn (see 'The Táin', page 22). Two foals are born at precisely the same moment as the hero, emphasizing his exalted status, and these are given to him as a present. The second episode concerns the curse of Macha. She was actually a war goddess, one of the incarnations of the Morrígán, but there are also clear equine associations. Her curse comes about as the result of a horse-race — an event that was specifically linked with the horse goddess, Epona (see page 59). It is no coincidence, moreover, that Cú Chulainn's horse is named the 'Grey of Macha'.

Some of these themes are reprised in the tales from *The Mabinogion*. It is noticeable, for example, that Pwyll's son, Pryderi (see 'Pwyll Encounters Rhiannon', page 104), is also born on the same night as a splendid foal. Like Cú Chulainn, too, the child grows up very quickly and displays prodigious strength for his age. The resemblance may not end there. For, according to one of the many theories about this slightly garbled tale, Pwyll's exchange with a lord of the Otherworld may orginally have occurred after he had married. During Pwyll's absence, this outsider would have sired Pryderi, in much the same way that Lugh fathered Cú Chulainn on the woman that he had spirited away from her mortal husband. The same Otherworld lord then returns to reclaim his child on the eve of Beltane, a time when the barriers between the real and the spiritual worlds are broken down. This provides a feasible reason for the abduction of the child, which is never satisfactorily explained in the Welsh version.

The character of Rhiannon, also featured in the tale of Pwyll, contains further references to a horse cult. Most commentators accept that she is related to the horse goddess, Epona. This is confirmed partly by her magical white mount, which no mortal can catch, and partly by the crudely appropriate nature of her punishment. Interestingly enough, the first of these details appears again, in the story about St Efflam (see page 142). Here, the magical horse is used entirely out of context, ridden by the saint's wife, but it does at least illustrate that the Breton chronicler had ready access to Celtic sources from across the Channel.

The Atlantis myth

If we consider another of the Celts' favourite themes, the same process can be seen working in reverse. Storytellers in Ireland, Wales and Brittany have all described a fabulous city that exists beneath the waves. In Irish lore, the place is not known as Atlantis but goes by several names. It is Tir fa Tonn, the marvellous submerged court that Diarmaid visits during one of his adventures; it is also the sunken island of Fincara, in *The Fate of the Children of Turenn*, and the unnamed city glimpsed in *The Voyage of Maildun*. In Welsh tradition, the tone changes. The flooded site is no longer an underwater paradise, but a disaster area. The entire cantred of Gwaelod, a district containing sixteen low-lying cities, becomes submerged when a drunken steward neglects the dyke protecting it. This region was ruled by Gwyddno Garanhir, the lord who is featured in 'The Birth of Taliesin' (see page 124). Because of his terrible loss, he was reduced to making his living from the fishing weir, where his son, Elphin, discovered the infant Taliesin.

These earlier versions of the story were greatly expanded and completely transformed in the Breton story of Ys. Here, the sinking of the city is unquestionably viewed as a disaster, but traces of the more optimistic Irish vision survive in some of the subsidiary myths. These suggest that life still goes on as normal in Ys, and that it will rise from the deep if certain conditions are fulfilled (if, for example, a diver can manage to ring the bell of Gradlon's church). The legend of Ys was touched upon by Marie de France, the twelfth-century authoress of the *Breton Lais*. However, fuller versions of this story also include a number of other influences: the familiar legend of a water-spirit falling in love with a mortal, the conversion of a pagan king, and also a European variation of the story of Sodom and Gomorrah.

The Arthurian link

Of course, no story unified the various Celtic traditions as completely as that of King Arthur. Many authorities have cited elements in the early Irish sagas, which are said to prefigure his exploits. Thus, Finn is seen as an early version of Arthur, while the story of Diarmaid and Gráinne is supposed to have served as a model for the romance of Tristram and Iseult. Similarly, comparisons are made between Suibhne Geilt and Merlin. There is also the celebrated tale where the sorcerer steals a stone circle known as the Giant's Dance and uses it to make Stonehenge. Another less slanderous version of the legend relates that Merlin entered the circle by moonlight and began to play his harp so sweetly, that the stones came to life and danced across the Irish Sea of their own accord.

The Arthurian sections in *The Mabinogion* are even more remarkable. In 'How Culhwch Won Olwen', probably the oldest tale in the collection, we gain one of our earliest sightings of the hero. He is already a king, but his court is situated at Kelli Wig in Cornwall. As a character, Arthur appears to be well established, suggesting that there may have been earlier stories that are now lost. Even so, he plays a comparatively minor role in the proceedings, outshone by two of his followers, Kai (later Sir Kay) and Bedwyr (later Sir Bedivere). These colourful creations are very different from the courtly figures that were to emerge in the later Arthurian romances. In spirit, their strange gifts and supernatural prowess bring them much closer to Cú Chulainn and his companions, than to any of the knights described by Malory or Chrétien de Troyes.

The tale of Peredur (see 'Peredur, Son of Evrawc', page 114) is considerably later and can certainly be classified as a romance. The eponymous hero has many affinities with Sir Perceval, and there are several links with the quest for the Holy Grail. The most notable of these are Peredur's lame uncle, who can probably be identified with the crippled Fisher King, and the tantalizing vision of the Holy Lance and the Grail itself, which Peredur witnesses in his castle.

Outside *The Mabinogion*, most Welsh associations with the Arthurian tradition are centred around Merlin. According to legend, he was born at Carmarthen (or 'Caer Myrddin', the earlier form of his name) and it is no accident that the modern eisteddfod movement was launched there. Brittany also boasts of close connections with the wizard. There, Merlin is said to have fashioned the Round Table for Arthur and there, too, in the Forest of Brocéliande, he is said to have met the enchantress Vivian. Tradition relates that he remains there to this day, held captive by her in an invisible prison.

Christian influences

Most of the relevant material from Brittany, however, stems from the end of the Celtic era, when the region was being converted to Christianity. Thus, the Arthur who aids St Efflam has become a slayer of dragons, which were seen as conventional symbols of paganism. Conversely, the old Celtic legends are linked increasingly with the missionaries who crossed the Channel, during the large-scale migrations of the fifth and sixth centuries. Initially, these evangelists worked in virtual isolation, adapting as well as they could to local conditions and beliefs. So, in the absence of strict regulation by the Church authorities, storytellers interlaced the accounts of their lives with anecdotes from pagan lore. This is how St Gildas came to own a magical ring, and how St Efflam was able to create a healing spring. The dividing line between Christian miracle and Celtic wizardry could be very slender.

Alongside the new saintly heroes, chroniclers also touched on the dilemma of the dying breed of druids and bards. Near the start of *The Barzaz Breiz*, there is a song attributed to Gwenc'hlan the bard who, blinded and imprisoned by his Christian tormentors, dreams of a day when the streets will run with their blood. Merlin, by contrast, is more philosophical, and he agrees to be converted. Merlin's attitude is more pragmatic than that of the druid in the story of the city of Ys, who simply retreats into the forest in the awareness that he can no longer stem the tide of the new religion. This elegiac note is echoed in a late addition to the Fionn Cycle, where Cailte, one of the few survivors of the fianna, journeys around Ireland accompanied by St Patrick, showing him the sites of some of their old exploits.

In spite of the nostalgic tone of these later works, the Celtic tradition did not vanish entirely. The various Arthurian cycles kept it alive throughout the Middle Ages, although it was much distorted. Then, during the Renaissance, the rediscovery of classical authors awakened new interest in the early inhabitants of Europe. Unfortunately, the highly-coloured accounts in some of these sources presented a misleading picture. As a result, one of the first studies about druids was published with a lurid frontispiece, showing sacrificial altars, piles of headless corpses, and a sinister priestess beating a drum with a human thigh-bone. Other authors were influenced by John White's drawings of American Indians, recently brought back from the New World, using them to portray their own ancestors as naked, painted savages.

Signs of a more positive outlook on Celtic history became increasingly apparent in the eighteenth century. In the 1720s, a dedicated antiquary named William Stukeley began work on his influential study of British megalithic sites, convinced that the stones of these landscapes had originally been designed as ancient Celtic temples. These ideas were eventually published in his books on Stonehenge (1740) and Avebury (1743). Similar moves were also afoot on the other side of the Channel, where scholars were warming to the view that Gaulish druids had been responsible for their prehistoric monuments.

Romantic fiction

The growing popularity of these notions may have helped to inspire the extraordinary literary hoax that pushed the Celts to the forefront of European consciousness. In 1760, a Scottish schoolmaster named James Macpherson published his *Fragments of Ancient Poetry translated from Gaelic and Erse*. This volume purported to be an anthology of third-century poems written by Ossian (the Scottish form of Oisin). The book was an immediate success, and the schoolmaster-turned-author rapidly followed it up with two epics: *Fingal* (1762), which recounted the adventures of Finn mac Cumhaill, and *Temora* (1763).

Macpherson claimed that he had 'collected' all this material in the course of his travels in the Highlands of Scotland. Literary experts were suspicious, none more so than Dr Johnson, who immediately declared the books to be fraudulent. This, however, did nothing to diminish the popularity of the texts; nor did it in any way harm Macpherson's reputation. In his later life, he was elected as a Member of Parliament. A full investigation into the authenticity of the works was only undertaken after his death, when it was agreed that they had been fabricated by the author from fragments of Irish ballads.

In a sense, though, the literary status of these books is irrelevant. Whether genuine or not, the Ossian collection proved enormously influential. They constituted a major landmark in the Romantic movement and they have coloured our perception of the Celtic world ever since. Goethe and Blake expressed their admiration for them, while Napoleon declared them to be his favourite books. He carried a volume with him on his campaigns and kept it by him, when he was exiled to St Helena. Artists and musicians were equally inspired by the forgery. Ingres painted a suitably misty version of *The Dream of Ossian* (1813) for Napoleon's bedroom in the Quirinal, while Anne-Louis Girodet's canvas of *Ossian Receiving the Warriors of the French Revolution into Paradise* (1801) was more grandiose still.

The interest created by Macpherson's book also encouraged the development of more serious research into the subject. The French set up an Académie Celtique in 1805, and archaeological studies were further stimulated by the discovery of a Celtic hoard, at Podmokly in Bohemia, in 1771. Here, the prize find was a cauldron filled with gold coins.

The search for genuine Celtic texts also intensified, following the revelations about James Macpherson's trickery. Individual stories from *The Mabinogion* were translated into English as early as 1795, while Lady Charlotte Guest's complete edition of the Welsh legends was published in three volumes, between 1838 and 1849. Hersart de la Villemarqué was working on *The Barzaz Breiz* at precisely the same time, publishing his results in 1839. For many years, however, the critics were sceptical of Villemarqué's book, fearing that it might prove to be as bogus as the Ossian texts. Recent research, however, has proved that it is a genuine collection.

The Celtic revival

In Ireland, the Celtic revival dates from the middle of the nineteenth century. The Irish Archaeological Society, founded in 1840, and the Celtic Society (1845) were both established to protect the nation's ancient monuments. Appropriately enough, this was rapidly followed by the discovery of two of Ireland's most famous treasures, the Tara Brooch (1850) and the Ardagh Chalice (1868). The Tara Brooch was found on the beach at Bettystown (the association with Tara was a romantic invention by an early owner), while the Ardagh Chalice was unearthed by a boy digging for potatoes. The former, in particular, captured the public imagination. It was exhibited at the Great Exhibition of 1851 and facsimile copies were soon being marketed. Queen Victoria is known to have purchased two of these.

The early Irish texts began to reach a wider audience at the end of the century, when a number of new translations and editions appeared. Perhaps the most accessible of these was *Cuchulain of Muirthemne* (1902), a spirited retelling of the *Táin* by Yeats' friend, Lady Gregory. Yeats himself provided a glowing preface to the book, describing how it encapsulated the ancient heart of Ireland. He also drew considerable inspiration from early Celtic material in his own work. His lengthy narrative poem, 'The Wanderings of Oisin' (1888), and *Diarmuid and Grania*, a play he wrote with George Moore, are characteristic examples.

The popularity of Celtic ideas, designs and traditions has continued to grow right throughout the twentieth century. In the design world, perhaps one of the most prominent marketers of 'Celtic style' was Liberty's of London. In the years leading up to the First World War, the store commissioned and introduced an entire range of 'Celtic' products, from mirrors and candlesticks to tea-sets and cigarette cases. A cursory glance at any craft store, jeweller's or market will confirm that the trend has mushroomed enormously since then.

In the field of music, too, the term 'Celtic' has become well nigh ubiquitous. Traditional material has featured strongly in the various folk revivals since the war, and there are some performers who have drawn more direct inspiration from the ancient texts of the Celts. The band Horslips, for example, recorded an ambitious concept album entitled 'The Táin' in 1974, and many groups have chosen to use evocative Celtic names, such as Epona, Cruachan and Barzaz.

In recent years, the Celtic tradition has also gained wider acceptance through the New Age movement. In their quest for an alternative lifestyle, this disparate group of enthusiasts has produced new and often unexpected interpretations of the Celtic past, using them to explore such fields as divination, mysticism and neo-paganism.

IRELAND

THE ANCIENT CELTS once flourished in most of Europe but it is in Ireland that their traditions have been most preserved. The early Irish chronicles conjure up a society dominated by an aristocratic warrior caste in an age before Christianity. The heroes of these epic tales prize nothing higher than fame and courage, as they battle the magical forces pitted against them. Their deeds are as noble and as mysterious as the hill-forts and standing stones that are scattered around the Irish landscape, while their boasts and love of exaggeration can compete with the most extravagant modern-day blarney.

THE TÁIN BÓ CUAILNGE

THE MOST IMPORTANT collection of early Irish stories is contained in the Ulster Cycle which narrates the exploits of Ulster's King Conchobar and hero-warrior, Cú Chulainn. The centrepiece of this cycle is the *Táin Bó Cuailnge*, or Cattle Raid of Cooley, which begins with the argument between Medb and Ailill and reaches a climax in the final battle. The remaining tales in the cycle act as a prologue to the raid, and expand other areas of the narrative.

This epic legend was transmitted orally during the fourth and fifth centuries, and it was first written down in the eighth or ninth century. The scribe was probably one of the *filidh*; Irish poet-scholars who specialized in storytelling. The story has survived in piecemeal fashion in a number of later manuscripts, principally *The Book of the Dun Cow*, *The Book of Leinster* and *The Yellow Book of Lecan*.

The *Táin* presents us with a unique picture of pre-Christian society in western Europe: ruled by an aristocratic warrior caste, politics and diplomacy hold no place. Individual fighting prowess is highly prized, and inter-tribal warfare is the order of the day. Cattle raids were commonplace and several are mentioned in the early sagas. The *Táin* was by far the most elaborate of these.

THE PLOT

Medb, Queen of Connacht, argues with her husband about their respective wealth. Discovering that his is the greater, she decides to redress the balance by seizing the Bull of Cooley, held by Conchobar, ruler of Ulster. He is unwilling to part with it, however, so Medb gathers an army to take it by force. Her plan seems likely to succeed, since the men of Ulster are weakened by a curse and are unable to fight. Unfortunately for Medb, the Ulster warrior Cú Chulainn is unaffected by this curse and he singlehandedly holds the forces of Connacht at bay. He performs remarkable feats of valour – but can he survive long enough for the army of Ulstermen to recover their strength?

THE CHARACTERS

Cú Chulainn The supreme warrior who defends Ulster against the men of Connacht.

Ferdia Friend of Cú Chulainn, now enlisted in the army of Connacht.

Scáthach The supernatural female warrior who trains Cú Chulainn and gives him his most fearsome weapon, the Gae Bolga.

Morrigán A shape-shifting war goddess.

Conchobar The king of Ulster and leader of the campaign against Medb and Ailill.

Medb (Maeve) The Queen of Connacht. Her greed sparks off the war with Ulster.

Ailill Medb's consort, the King of Connacht.

Fergus Mac Roth A former king of Ulster, who defects to the court of Medb and Ailill.

Macha A war goddess associated with the Morrigán. She has placed a curse on the men of Ulster, weakening them greatly during the ensuing conflict.

Emer The wife of Cú Chulainn.

CÚ CHULAINN'S YOUTH

OW IT HAPPENED ON a certain day that Conchobar, the King of Ulster, was at his capital, Emain Macha, preparing for the marriage of his sister Dechtire. She was to wed a prince named Sualtam, the brother of Fergus Mac Roth. At the wedding feast, Dechtire grew thirsty and took some wine. But, as she was drinking it, a mayfly flew into the cup and she swallowed it along with the wine. Soon after, she went into the parlour with her fifty maidens and fell into a sleep. And in this sleep, Lugh the god of light appeared before her, saying: 'I was that mayfly that came into your cup. Now you and your maidens must follow me.' Whereupon, he transformed them all into of a flock of birds and they travelled south with him, to the fairy-dwelling at Brugh na Bóinne. Here they remained, and no one at Emain Macha knew where they were.

About a year later, Conchobar and his nobles were gathered again at Emain Macha, attending another feast. Suddenly, they spied through the window a great flock of birds, which proceeded to descend onto the plain and feed upon the crops. They ravaged the land, leaving behind them not so much as a blade of grass.

The men of Ulster were sorely vexed when they saw the birds destroying all the crops that lay in their path. Swiftly, they yoked up their chariots and began to pursue them. Conchobar led the way and Fergus Mac Roth and poison-tongued Bricriu were among the company. The chase took them south and, as their chariots thundered through the open country, they could not help admiring the beauty of the birds. There were nine flocks of them in all, linked in pairs by chains of silver. And, at the head of each flock, there were two birds of different colours, linked together by a chain of gold. In front of all of these, there were three birds which flew alone, leading them all towards Brugh na Bóinne.

Darkness fell and the birds vanished from the sky. Conchobar ordered his men to dismount and sent Bricriu to seek out shelter. All he could find, however, was a poor-looking house, where an old couple made him welcome. They bade him bring his companions to share their hospitality, but Bricriu was unimpressed with what was on offer. When he returned to Conchobar, he said that there would be little point in accepting the offer, unless they took their own provisions along.

Despite this, the men of Ulster went with Conchobar to the house. To their surprise, they found that it was large and well-appointed, and completely different to Bricriu's description. At the door, they were greeted by a young man with a shining countenance, dressed in a suit of armour. He ushered them in and led them to the feasting table. Food and drink of every kind awaited them there and the lords of Ulster wasted no time in satisfying their appetites. When they had consumed every morsel, Conchobar turned to the young man and enquired after his lady: 'Where is the mistress of the house that she does not come to bid us welcome?'

'You cannot see her tonight,' was the reply, 'for she is in the pangs of childbirth.' And sure enough, later that night, the bawl of a newborn infant could be heard throughout the house. At the very same moment, a mare also gave birth to two foals in the field outside. And the men of Ulster took charge of the foals, meaning to present them as a gift for the new child.

In the morning, Conchobar was the first to rise. He went to look for his host, but the man was nowhere to be seen. So, hearing the cry of a baby, he went to the mother's room. There he found Dechtire, with her maidens all around her and a child lying in her lap. And she welcomed Conchobar and explained to him all that had occurred; how she and her maidens had been spirited away from Emain Macha by Lugh, and how he had appeared before the Ulstermen as a young man dressed in armour.

Conchobar listened to all that was said, and was delighted to find his sister safe and well after so long an absence. And he praised her, saying: 'You have done well, Dechtire. You have given shelter to me and my chariots; you have kept the cold from my horses; you have given food to me and my people; and now you bring us this child, the finest gift of all.'

The news was swiftly passed to the men of Ulster. They, too, were pleased about the baby, offering to raise the child and instruct him in their own special skills. As their arguments became very fierce, Conchobar decided they should return to Emain to consult Morann, the judge, on the matter. His words were always held in high esteem because the torc round his neck would tighten if he gave a false judgment. So it was agreed, and the company travelled back to Emain.

When they arrived there, Morann made his judgment. 'It is for Conchobar to raise the child, for he is next of kin to him. But let Sencha the poet instruct him in speech and oratory; let Fergus the warrior hold him on his knees; and let Amergin the sage be his tutor.' And he added: 'This child will be praised by all, by chariot drivers and soldiers, by kings and seers. He will avenge all your wrongs; he will defend your fords and fight all your battles.'

And so it was settled. The child was taken to the plain of Muirthemne, where he spent his infant years with Dechtire and her husband Sualtam, before passing into the care of Conchobar. And the name they gave him was Setanta.

It did not take long for Setanta to show signs of the prowess that Morann had prophesied. On one occasion, while still an infant, he was roused from his sleep by a serving man and struck the fellow such a fierce blow that the

man's forehead was pushed into his brain. After this, no one dared to wake him unexpectedly. Then, when he was just seven, Setanta, later called Cú Chulainn, joined the boy troop of Ulster on the hurling-field, treating his playmates so roughly that they had to ask him for his protection. Soon, his strength would lead him on to greater exploits.

In Ulster, there was a smith named Culann, who offered to prepare a feast for Conchobar and his people. Since he was not a man of property and had no great riches, Culann asked the king if he could limit the number of guests he brought with him. 'Willingly,' said Conchobar, and in his train he brought just fifty chariots, carrying the finest and the mightiest of his subjects.

As he was leaving for the feast, Conchobar passed the hurling-field, where Setanta was playing at ball with the boy troop of Ulster. As usual, the child outshone all those around him. Thrice fifty came against him, but Setanta evaded their challenges each time and drove the ball into the goal. Conchobar marvelled at the youngster's skill and called him over, bidding him join the company at the smith's feast. 'I cannot come now,' Setanta replied, 'for these boys have not yet had their fill of play. But I will follow the chariot tracks and join you later.'

So Conchobar went to the smith's house, where he was made welcome. Fresh rushes were laid on the ground, and songs and poems were recited. Soon, the feast was brought in and the guests began to gorge themselves. At this point, Culann turned to the king and asked: 'Will any more of your people be joining us tonight?'

'They will not,' replied Conchobar, forgetting his invitation to Setanta.

'Then I will loose my fierce hound into the fields outside the house,' explained the smith. 'He

ANIMAL SYMBOLISM

THE SYMBOLIC significance of animals is apparent in every aspect of Celtic life. Evidence has shown that a wide variety of creatures were used in sacrifices and in certain funerary rites. In addition, animal imagery is an ever-present feature in artworks and literature. The bull, as might be guessed from its prominence in the *Táin*, was a symbol of power and wealth. Tarvos Trigaranus, the three-horned bull, was revered both in Britain and Gaul and the beast was also associated with the selection of the high kings at Tara. Candidates had to participate in a Tarbhfhess, a ceremonial 'bull-sleep' presided over by druids.

Boars, too, featured in sacrifices and ritual feasting. They were more closely associated with war, however, and were frequently portrayed on shields and armour. Other animals were believed to possess special powers. Dogs, for example, were associated with healing, as their saliva was thought to have curative properties, while salmon were regarded as a source of knowledge. This is confirmed in a number of Irish and Welsh stories. In the Fionn cycle, Finn gains wisdom after tasting the flesh of the Salmon of Knowledge, while questing Welsh knights, in the tale of Culhwch and Olwen, enlist the aid of the Salmon of Llyn Llyw.

has the strength of a hundred curs and obeys no one but myself. He will keep us safe from any unexpected intruders.'

At Emain Macha, meanwhile, the boys of Ulster had finished their play and returned to their homes. So, keeping his promise, Setanta set out towards the feasting place. To pass the time, he amused himself by striking a silver ball with his hurling-stick and then casting the stick after it. Quick as the wind, he chased after them, catching both the ball and the stick before they reached the ground.

When Setanta drew near to the smith's house, the hound sensed him coming and gave out such a howl, that it could be heard throughout Ulster. Then it sprang up violently and opened its jaws so wide that it seemed as if it meant to swallow the youth whole.

Setanta had no weapons but his hurling-stick and his silver ball. So, when he saw the beast coming for him, he struck the ball with such force that it went straight down the dog's gullet and tore out its entrails. Then he seized the thing by its hind legs and dashed it against a rock, so that its limbs were ripped out of their sockets.

When the company inside heard all the commotion, they feared for the life of the intruder and Conchobar stood up in alarm, suddenly remembering his invitation to Setanta. 'Surely it was ill luck that brought us here tonight,' he said to the smith, 'for that must be my sister's child, who has met his death through your hound.' With this, the men of Ulster rose up from their seats, leaping over tables and whatever other obstacles blocked their path, as they hastened outside to see what had happened.

Fergus was first upon the scene, gathering Setanta up in his arms and carrying him back into the house. All rejoiced to see the lad safe and well. Only Culann was sorrowful, when he saw his hound lying dead and broken in the grass. 'It was ill luck that brought you here tonight,' he said to Setanta. 'The hound that you have taken from me was a valued member of my household, for he protected my herds, my flocks and all my goods. Without him, enemies will come and steal them from me and my livelihood will be ruined.'

'Do not be angry,' replied the boy, 'for I will make good the injury I have done you.'

'How can you possibly do that,' enquired the smith.

'I will find and rear a pup of the same breed, training it myself until it is just as fine as the hound you have lost. In the meantime, I myself will be your guard-dog, watching over your goods, your cattle and your house.'

'That is a very fair offer,' said Cathbad the Druid, 'I could not have thought of a better solution myself. And from this moment on, everyone will know you as Cú Chulainn, the Hound of Culann.'

'But I prefer my own name, Setanta son of Sualtam,' complained the boy.

'Do not say that,' Cathbad continued, 'for one day, every warrior in the world will come to know and fear the name of Cú Chulainn.'

'If that is the case,' replied the boy, 'then I am content to do as you say.' And that is how the name of Cú Chulainn came into being.

There came a time, not long after this, when Cathbad the Druid was instructing pupils in his house at Emain Macha. There were nine pupils, and one of these asked the sage to read the signs and tell them if the day held any special omens. 'Certainly,' replied Cathbad. 'The signs show that if any young man should take up arms this day, he will perform great feats of valour and his name will live forever in the annals of Ireland. His span of life, however, will be short.'

Now Cú Chulainn was playing outside Cathbad's house and overheard this remark. Immediately, he put down his hurling-stick and went to see Conchobar. Brimming over with excitement, he asked the king's permission to take up arms.

Conchobar was surprised by the boy's zeal. 'Who has put that idea into your head?' he enquired.

'Cathbad the Druid,' replied Cú Chulainn.

This answer satisfied the king. 'If Cathbad has recommended it, then I will not deny you,' he pronounced. Then he took the boy to his armoury and offered him his choice of weapons, from among those set aside for new warriors. Cú Chulainn tried them all, but he brandished them so fiercely that they were soon broken. Eventually, Conchobar presented him with his own arms — his two spears, his sword and his shield — and these pleased the young man.

Just at this moment, Cathbad the Druid entered the king's house and was fearful at what he saw. 'Is this young lad taking arms today?' he asked. Conchobar nodded.

'Then I grieve for his mother, for her son's life will soon be cut short.'

Conchobar was horrified. 'But did you yourself not advise him to take up arms today?'

'Most certainly, I did not,' replied the druid.

'Then you have lied to me, boy,' said Conchobar, turning towards Cú Chulainn.

'I told no lie,' he replied, 'for it was Cathbad who persuaded me to take arms today, when I overheard him talking to his pupils. It is true that he mentioned my life would be brief, but that is a small price to pay if the reward is undying honour.'

'Well,' said Cathbad, 'let us see if my prophecy was good. Step into a chariot now and show us what you can do.' Cú Chulainn obeyed and tried his mettle on the first chariot that he saw. But, as with the weapons earlier in the day, the equipment was unequal to the strength of its new owner and the frame broke and the chariot crashed to the ground. Twelve more chariots were broken in this way until, at length, Conchobar called for his own chariot. Cú Chulainn tried it and found it to his liking. 'This is the chariot that suits me,' he declared.

Conchobar summoned his personal charioteer, Jubair, and entrusted Cú Chulainn to his care. Jubair drove the lad a little way out of Emain, meaning to give him a safe trial of the chariot. But Cú Chulainn insisted on going further afield, into more dangerous territory. At last, they came to the most hazardous place of all, the fort belonging to the sons of Nechta Scéne.

'Are these the same men who happily boast that the number of

Ulstermen still living is less than the number that they have killed?'

'They are the very same men,' Jubair agreed.

On hearing this, Cú Chulainn climbed down from the chariot and approached the fort. On the grass near the entrance, there was a pillar-stone with an iron hoop around it. The hoop carried an inscription in Ogham, warning that any man bearing weapons in that place would be challenged to fight. Immediately, Cú Chulainn stretched his arms around the stone, uprooted it from the ground, and hurled it into a nearby river.

Jubair was scornful. 'I don't see that you have achieved much by that,' he said, 'except that it may bring you the early death that you appear to be seeking.'

Cú Chulainn ignored this remark and instructed the charioteer to spread out some skins on the chariot, so that he could sleep for a while. He also ordered that he should on no account be wakened. Jubair did as he was told, although he did remark that it was most unwise to choose to sleep on an enemy's land.

OGHAM

 OGHAM WAS THE ancient alphabet of the Celts. It is thought to have been invented in southern Ireland, although examples have been found in many parts of the British Isles. Letters were composed of straight or slanting lines, incised onto the edges of wooden or stone blocks. Evidence suggests that it was in common use from c. AD 300 until the seventh century, although some authorities believe that it may have been used even earlier on perishable materials. The Irish sagas tell of great libraries of ogham texts, recorded on pieces of bark, but no traces of these have been found. In the *Táin*, Cú Chulainn issued challenges to the Connacht men in ogham, carved on standing stones. The ogham was also believed to have magical properties, and druids used them in divination. The system was named after Ogma, the god of eloquence, prized by the Celts who rated word-power higher than physical prowess.

Shortly afterwards, while Cú Chulainn was sleeping, the three sons of Nechta Scéne arrived. 'Who is it,' called out one of them, 'that has dared to cross the border and come onto our land?'

'A young lad,' replied Jubair, 'who has just taken arms today and is not worthy of your enmity.'

'He has made an unfortunate choice for his first expedition,' replied one of the brothers. 'Take him and go. Graze your horses here no more.'

'The reins are already in my hand,' said Jubair, making ready to go. 'Besides, he is not old enough to fight. He is just a child, who should be in his father's house.'

But Cú Chulainn had woken up and was filled with fury, on hearing this insult. 'He is not a child at all,' he cried out, 'but one who has come here in search of combat. Let us go down to the ford and I will prove it.'

'With pleasure!' came the reply. And the first of the sons of Nechta Scéne made his way down to the river.

'You must beware of this one,' warned Jubair. 'His name is Foill and you must kill him with your first stroke. Otherwise, you will have no chance of ever defeating him, even if you fight together all day.'

'Do not worry,' said Cú Chulainn. 'I swear by the oath of my people that he won't try his tricks on an Ulsterman again.' So saying, he took hold of Conchobar's great spear, the Venomous, and hurled it at the man. And the spear passed through Foill's shield, broke three of his ribs and cut straight through his heart. Then Cú Chulainn took up his sword and cut the man's head off, before the body had fallen to the ground. He took this and Foill's weapons as trophies, handing them to Jubair for safe-keeping.

'You must take care of this one,' warned the charioteer, as the next man advanced. 'His name is Fainnle, nicknamed the Swallow, for he travels through water with the nimble manner of a bird and no swimmer can catch him. But Cú Chulainn was undaunted, swearing only that the man would never have the chance to play such tricks again. Then he joined Fainnle in the river and, even though his feet could not touch the bottom, he wrestled with the man and took his head off with a blow of his sword. Cú Chulainn carried this trophy back to the water's edge, allowing the headless trunk to drift away downstream.

'Now really beware of this man,' said Jubair, as the last son of Nechta Scéne came towards them. 'His name is Túachell and he cannot be felled by any spear or sword.'

'So much the worse for him,' declared Cú Chulainn, and instead he lifted up a large rock and hurled it at his foe. The rock was thrown with such force that it passed right through the man's skull, leaving a hole the size of a fist. Once again, he cut off the head and seized the weapons of his adversary, taking them back to Jubair. A sad wailing could be heard coming from the fort, as Nechta Scéne grieved for the loss of her three sons. Cú Chulainn remained unmoved, however, swearing that he would keep hold of his trophies until he returned to Emain Macha.

On the journey back, Cú Chulainn trapped a stag and twenty swans, tying them to his chariot. His triumphal return, with the birds flying overhead and the mens' severed heads dangling from the side of the chariot, made a great impression on Conchobar's people.

As Cú Chulainn grew towards manhood, his skills in the arts of war became a source of wonder at Emain Macha. All the women of Ulster loved him for his strength, his handsome features and his fine way of speaking. They also admired his wisdom, his prudence in battle and his gifts of prophecy and judgment. Indeed, they could only find three faults in him – that he was too young, too brave and too beautiful.

The men of Ulster became concerned about Cú Chulainn's popularity and resolved to find a wife for him. Once he was married, they reasoned, there would be less danger of him turning the heads of their wives and daughters. Besides, they knew of the prophecy that he was to die young and thought it a shame that so great a warrior should leave no heir behind him. So, Conchobar sent nine men into each of the provinces of Ireland, to seek out a suitable mate for their hero. They looked in every town and every fort but, at the end of the year, they returned to Emain Macha empty-handed.

Then Cú Chulainn himself went out to a place named Luglochta Loga, the Garden of Lugh. There, he met with a girl that he already knew. Her name was Emer, the daughter of Forgall Manach the Cunning. Of all the girls in Ireland, she was the most suitable; for she had the six gifts – the gift of beauty, the gift of voice, the gift of sweet words, the gift of wisdom, the gift of needlework and the gift of chastity.

When Cú Chulainn arrived, Emer was sitting in the field with her maidens, schooling them in their needlework. She recognized him instantly, greeting him with these words: 'May the gods make all roads smooth before you.'

CELTIC WEAPONS

THE CELTS WERE renowned for their fighting prowess, so it is hardly surprising that they placed a high value on fine weaponry. Iron-working had been introduced during the Hallstatt period and, by the sixth century BC, warriors were using heavy, long-bladed slashing swords. Many had richly decorated hilts, inlaid with amber, ivory or gold-leaf. Scabbards, shields and helmets were similarly decorated. At a very early stage, a clear distinction was made between functional weaponry and parade gear. The latter was highly ornamental, but usually too fragile to withstand genuine warfare. Dead warrior princes were sometimes laid on the back of a chariot, sword in hand, and weapons were deliberately discarded as a form of sacrifice in lakes or rivers. There is a likely echo of this practice in the way that Excalibur, King Arthur's sword, was cast into the water at the time of his death. Naming weapons and attributing special powers to them was typical of the Celts. Fergus' magic sword 'Cladcholg', which may be related to Excalibur, was said to stretch the whole length of a rainbow and slice the tops off hills. Similarly, in the *Táin*, the hero Cú Chulainn wields the 'Gae Bolga', an awesome spear presented to him by Scáthach, his supernatural combat tutor.

'And you,' he replied, 'may you keep safe from every harm.' After this, they began to speak in riddles, so that the maidens would not understand them. And in their double-talk, Cú Chulainn made it plain to Emer that he wished to make her his wife.

His eyes observed the rise of her breasts above the top of her dress. 'That is a fair country,' he said. 'How I might wish to wander there.'

Emer smiled, 'No man may travel there, unless he kills a hundred men at every ford between Ailbine and Banchuig Arcait.'

Cú Chulainn looked at her again and said, 'That is a fair country.'

Emer then replied: 'No man may travel there, until he has slain thrice nine men with a single stroke, sparing a single man in each group of nine.'

Once more, Cú Chulainn looked at her and repeated, 'That is a fair country.'

Emer spoke again saying: 'No man may travel there, who has not gone sleepless from Samhain to the lambing time at Imbolc, and from Imbolc to the fiery season of Beltane, then again from Beltane to Lughnasadh, when the earth yields up its fruit, and then finally round to Samhain time again.'

'Everything shall be as you command,' agreed Cú Chulainn.

'Then I accept the offer you have made me,' said Emer. And, with these riddling words, Cú Chulainn took his leave and returned to Emain Macha.

After his departure, Emer's maidens went home and told their parents about the strange conversation they had witnessed. Their words, in turn, were reported to Forgall Manach and, although he could not understand the hidden meanings of their speech, he was suspicious of Cú Chulainn's motives. So, determined to hinder the boy's plans, he donned the disguise of a Gaulish chieftain and travelled to Emain Macha. There, he was warmly received by Conchobar and the men of Ulster.

For three days, there was feasting and drinking and, during this time, Forgall praised the fighting skills of his hosts. Above all, he praised Cú Chulainn for his feats and daring, adding that the young man would be well advised to journey to the island of Scáthach the Shadowy One. For surely, once he had completed his training under this great female warrior, no one in the world would dare to cross swords with him. Cú Chulainn leapt at the idea and promised to set out the very next day. Forgall smiled at this, for it was his hope that the young man would perish on the dangerous route to the Isle of Shadows, and would never return to marry his daughter.

Cú Chulainn's expedition to Scáthach's island proved just as hazardous as Forgall had anticipated. New troubles beset him at every stage of the journey. He came through every test, however, finally reaching his goal. After conversing with Scáthach's daughter, Uathach, for three days, she advised Cú Chulainn to ask three wishes of her mother. He asked her for three things: to be taught the craft of arms, to have a dowry for his wedding, and to have some knowledge of his future, as Scáthach had the gift of prophecy. Scáthach taught him many skills such as how to perform the hero's salmon-leap, how to stand

on a lance-point and how to drive the sickle-chariot. She also gave him his most fearsome weapon, the Gae Bolga, which made only one wound when entering the body and then expanded into thirty more beneath the flesh. Armed with his new-found weapon and new battle skills, Cú Chulainn began the long journey back to Emain Macha, determined to claim his bride.

Cú Chulainn's safe return was greeted with astonishment by Forgall. For, while the youth had been absent, he had betrothed his daughter, Emer, to Lugaid, a king of Munster. So, Forgall and his sons made strong their fort at Luglochta Loga and kept a close watch on Emer.

For a whole year, Cú Chulainn did not even manage to catch a brief glimpse of her. And, throughout this period, he could not go to sleep. Neither from the snows of Samhain to the

IMBOLC

IMBOLC WAS THE second of the Celtic seasonal festivals, covering the months of February, March and April. The chief rituals were carried out on 1 February and had strong associations with fertility. In pastoral terms, they were linked with lambing and the lactation of ewes. The festival was also devoted to the powerful triple-goddess, Brigid. In her different aspects, she was influential in the fields of healing, poetry and smithcraft. Poets regarded her as the source of literary inspiration and her protection was frequently invoked by mothers in childbirth. In Ireland, she was much revered by the filidh (sages), who recognized her gift of prophecy. The cult of Brigid was probably connected with the worship of Brigantia, a northern British deity, and also with the Irish saint of the same name. It can be no coincidence that the latter's feast day is celebrated on 1 February, the same day as Imbolc.

lambing time at Imbolc, nor from Imbolc to the day of the fires at Beltane; neither from Beltane to Lughnasadh when the crops were gathered in, nor even in the final months, when the seasons turned again to Samhain time. And so it was in this way, that Cú Chulainn managed to fulfil the first of Emer's difficult conditions.

At length, when the year had ended, Cú Chulainn harnessed up his sickle-chariot and drove towards Forgall's fort in earnest. There, he performed his salmon-leap, bounding over the triple walls of its defences to reach the central enclosure.

Next, he made three attacks into Forgall's stronghold. In each of these, he killed eight men, leaving a ninth man to run away unharmed. And the survivors from these attacks were the men named Scibar, Ibor and Cat, the three brothers of Emer. Therefore, in this manner, Cú Chulainn fulfilled the second of her conditions.

Then Cú Chulainn hurriedly made his way to Emer's chamber, carrying her away from her father's house. Cú Chulainn and Emer also took with them Emer's foster-sister and two wagon-loads of gold and silver, which matched the weight of the two sisters. But Forgall sent men after them, pursuing them as far as Scenmend's Ford. There, his men caught up with the lovers and Cú Chulainn turned to face them. In the ensuing battle, he slew one hundred men, before the couple managed to escape and continue along the river towards Emain Macha.

However, Forgall's men soon caught up with them again. This time it was at a place called Glondáth, Ford of the Deed. Once more, Cú Chulainn made ready for battle, unsheathed his sword and reddened the earth with the blood of his foes. At last, when the fighting subsided, one hundred of Forgall's warriors lay dead at the river's edge.

On several more occasions, Emer and Cú Chulainn were overtaken by Forgall's men, and Cú Chulainn had to set about them with his weapons. It happened at the fords of Crúfóit, Raeban and Ath na Imfuait. In short, it happened at every ford along the river Boyne, between Ailbine and Banchuig Arcait. At each of these places Cú Chulainn easily slew a hundred men at a time and, by achieving this, he fulfilled the last and most challenging of the conditions that Emer had stipulated.

By nightfall, Cú Chulainn and Emer safely reached Emain Macha. There, they received a warm and hearty welcome from all the chiefs of Ulster. And after much feasting and rejoicing, Cú Chulainn was finally allowed to take Emer for his wife, and King Conchobar paid Emer's dowry. It was not long before all the difficulties they had faced together during their long courtship were forgotten, and they remained living happily together until death separated them.

THE PLOT TO STEAL THE BULL

T HAPPENED ONCE, when Ailill and Queen Medb were in their royal bedchamber at Cruachan, that they fell into an argument. This is how the dispute began:

'It is true what they say,' declared Ailill, 'that a rich man's wife certainly enjoys a comfortable life.'

'No doubt that is true,' replied Medb, 'but I am curious as to what exactly makes you mention it just now?'

'I was just thinking,' Ailill continued, 'how much better off you are today with me, than on the day I married you.'

'But you know that my situation was just as properous, before I even set eyes upon you,' protested Medb vehemently.

'That's not what I heard,' replied Ailill. 'You only had women's trinkets, and what little wealth you did possess was carried off by neighbouring enemies.'

'That's not how it was at all,' retorted Medb. 'My father was Eochaid, king of Ireland, and of his six daughters I was held in the highest esteem. I was the best at fighting and the most generous. I had fifteen hundred soldiers in my pay and fifteen hundred more: the sons of my chieftains. On top of this, my father gave me a province of Ireland, Cruachan, to rule as my own.'

'As for suitors,' she continued, 'I was wooed by your brother Finn, the king of Leinster; by Cairbre Niafer, the king of Tara; by Conchobar, the powerful king of Ulster; and by Eochu Beag, the son of Luchta. All of these men I refused, for I had set my heart on a dowry that few could offer. I wanted a husband who would be without fear, jealousy or miserliness, and I found him in you. A man without these qualities would have lived in my shadow, scorned by others for having a wife who was braver and more generous than himself.'

'And when I chose you, I showered you with the finest wedding gifts. I gave you enough apparel for a dozen men, a splendid chariot worth thrice seven serving-maids, the width of your face in red gold, and the span of your arm in white bronze. So, if anyone should bring shame or sorrow upon you, I am the one who should feel slighted, for you are nothing more than a kept man.'

Ailill was badly stung by these words. 'That is a lie. I am the son of a king and I also have two brothers who are kings – Finn of Leinster and Cairbre of Tara. They rule only because they are older than me, not because they are more worthy. It is true that you hold this province, but it is the only one in Ireland governed by a woman. I claim kingship over it, not through you, but through my mother, Mata of Muiresc, who was the daughter of Mágach of Connacht.'

'The fact remains,' said Medb, 'that my riches far outweigh yours.'

'Never,' cried Ailill. 'No one in Ireland has a better store of jewels and treasure than I.'

'Very well, let us put that to the test,' Medb challenged. 'Let all our goods be brought out and valued and then we will know, once and for all, who is the richer.'

'Agreed,' said Ailill and, with that, the inventory began. First, they brought out all their lowlier possessions: their drinking vessels, their vats and all their household goods. These were found to be equal. Next, they brought out their jewels and finery. Majestic were the rings, the brooches and the bracelets that passed before their eyes. Then came their apparel, all made of the finest cloth and in an infinite array of colours. Here, too, no difference could be found between their respective fortunes.

Then came the turn of their beasts. Great flocks of sheep were driven in from the fields and counted. Once again, though, there was parity between them. Even Medb's great ram, which alone was worth the price of a serving-maid, was matched by a similar beast in Ailill's flocks. The same was true of the horses that were brought in from the meadows and the pigs that were gathered in from the woods and gullies. Finally, the last comparison of all was made between their herds of cattle, which were driven in from the forests and the wild places of the province. These, too, were similar, except in one crucial respect. For, among Medb's herds, there had been a massive bull, which people called Fionnbanach or 'the White-horned'. This bull, however, had thought it unseemly to be under the control of a woman and had thus gone across to join the herds of Ailill.

When Medb realized this, she was furious. For it was plain that this was the best bull in the whole of Connacht, and she had nothing in her herd to match it. Now, all her wealth counted for nothing. She placed no value in it, if it could not equal that of her husband.

Swiftly, Medb summoned her herald, Mac Roth, and asked him to find out if there was any bull in Ireland that could compare with the White-horned one. 'I can tell you that straight away,' answered Mac Roth. 'In Ulster, in the district of Cooley, Dáire, the son of Fachna, owns a Brown Bull that is twice as good as this one.'

'Go quickly, then,' Medb ordered, 'and ask Dáire if I can borrow his bull for a year. Tell him that, if he agrees, I will reward him well. His payment for the loan shall be fifty heifers, a fine stretch of land on the plain of Ai, a chariot to the value of thrice seven serving-maids and, most of all, my intimate friendship.'

Mac Roth obeyed his mistress, hurrying to Cooley to make the offer to Dáire. Initially, it was well received. Dáire was so pleased with the bargain that he agreed to let the bull be taken away that very day. Before Mac Roth and his company departed, they were shown great hospitality. Fresh rushes were laid and much food and drink was brought before the men. Soon, many of them were drunk and, in their cups, they spoke with greater freedom.

'The owner of this house is a good man,' said one of Mac Roth's messengers.

'Indeed, he is,' said a second. 'The only better man in this part of Ireland is Conchobar, the king of Ulster.'

'Do you not think it strange, though,' continued the first, 'that he willingly gave us the prize, which the fighting men of the four provinces of Ireland would have struggled to seize?'

'There's nothing odd in that,' said the second, 'for if

CELTIC DECORATION

Detail of the Battersea shield decorated with glass or enamel inlay in a stylized, symmetrical pattern.

THE MOST distinctive and unifying aspect of Celtic culture is its style of decoration. This developed during the early stages of the prehistoric La Tène period, when it featured primarily on metalwork and stonework, and it was still a potent force a millennium later, when scribes and illuminators came to create the great Gospel books. Simplicity and adaptability are the main reasons for this longevity. The essential components of Celtic design consist of a few basic shapes, including spirals, interlacing, fretwork and swastikas, which are woven together to form intricate patterns. Figurative elements are sometimes combined with these abstract forms, but they are always highly stylized, echoing the rhythms of the overall design. So, the limbs or beards of human figures may lock together, to form swastikas or triangles, while the bodies of birds or animals taper away into ribbon-like strands, which then become part of an interlacing pattern. Celtic craftsmen produced infinite variations on these themes, employing them in every possible medium. As a result, a knotwork pattern on a sword might be reproduced on a lavish item of jewellery or a sacred image in a manuscript.

Dáire had refused to hand over the bull, Medb and Ailill would have taken it by force.'

Now Dáire's steward was passing by and overheard these words. He reported them back to his master and Dáire turned red with anger. 'By the gods,' he roared, 'we'll soon find out if that is true.'

Nothing more was said and the messengers of Mac Roth rested happily that night. The next morning, however, when they came to ask Dáire where he kept the bull, they received an unpleasant surprise. He refused point blank to tell them, adding that they were lucky to be leaving Cooley with their lives. Mac Roth enquired why he had changed his mind and Dáire repeated the conversation that his steward had overheard.

'This is nothing,' argued Mac Roth. 'No one should pay any heed to the words of drunken fools.' But Dáire would not be moved and the herald was forced to return to Cruachan empty-handed. Medb was angry at the failure of the mission and demanded to know the reasons. Then, when Mac Roth had explained all, she made a resolution.

'So be it! If Dáire believes that I would take the bull by force, he shall soon discover the truth of his words. Taken it shall be!'

The Brown Bull of Cooley and the White-horned Bull of Cruachan were no ordinary creatures. This is how they came into being. There were once two pig-keepers called Friuch and Rucht. Friuch was in the service of Bodb of Munster, while Rucht's master was Ochall Ochne of Connacht. The two men had much in common. Their names reflected their posts – Friuch took his name from the bristles of a boar, while Rucht's resembled its grunt – and both men were well practised in the art of shape-shifting. They were also great friends. Whenever the oak mast and beech nuts in Connacht were plentiful, Friuch would bring his swine north to feed on them. Similarly, whenever the trees in Munster produced the finer crop, Rucht was made welcome in the south.

But, after a time, ill-wishers stirred up trouble between the two men. The people of Connacht argued that Rucht's powers were the greater, while those of Munster sided with their man. Rucht raised the topic during his next stay in Munster and, soon, the pair were arguing.

'Let us put it to the test,' said Friuch. 'I will cast a spell on your pigs and, however much they eat while they are in my province, they will remain lean and poor.' The swineherd was as good as his word and, while his own pigs grew fat as they fed off the mast, Rucht's pigs became thinner and weaker. When he drove them home, his countrymen jeered at the sorry state of his herd and Ochall Ochne dismissed Rucht from his service. 'This proves nothing,' Rucht muttered to himself. 'I'll take my revenge when Friuch next brings his herd to me.'

Sure enough, a year later, it was Friuch's turn to lead his pigs into the neighbouring province. Rucht cast a similar spell over them and the beasts remained thin and poor, no matter how much they ate. When Friuch returned home, he too was dismissed from his post.

35

But all this did not put an end to the swineherds' quarrel. They turned themselves into ravens and made a great cawing noise, scolding each other constantly. They spent a whole year in Connacht at the fort of Cruachan, squabbling in this way. Then they flew south to Munster, to continue with their bickering. Here, they were spotted by Ochall's steward, Findell.

'What a racket those birds are making,' he exclaimed. 'They sound as bad as the two we had in Cruachan last year.' With that, the ravens turned back into men and Findell greeted them, recognizing them as the shape-shifting swineherds.

'You do wrong to welcome us,' said Friuch, 'for we shall be the cause of many deaths. Wives shall weep for husbands, sisters shall weep for brothers, all on our account.'

Findell was deeply shocked by this gloomy prophecy and he tried to discover what lay behind it, asking the pig-keepers what they had been doing since their last meeting.

'We have been up to no good,' came the reply. 'Since you last saw us, we have been living in the shape of birds, pursuing our quarrel. We have been in these forms for two years and now we plan to change again, this time into water creatures.' Then, as Findell looked on, they underwent the promised transformation and slid into the water. They spent the next year in the river Siuir and the year after that in the river Sionnan, all the time attempting to devour each other.

But these were not the final transformations of Rucht and Friuch. Next, they turned themselves into war-mongering champions, urging men into battle. Four kings died in the conflicts they caused, and Ochall and Bodb were among them. Then they turned themselves into shadows, threatening each other, and many people just died of fright after witnessing their phantom shapes.

Eventually, the pig-keepers changed themselves into eels. One of them went into the river Cruind, in the district of Cooley, and there it was swallowed up by a cow belonging to Dáire, son of Fachna. The second eel, meanwhile, slipped into the spring of Uaran Garad in Connacht. Medb saw it there one day and fished it out of the water in a small bronze vessel. She gazed at it for a long time, since it was like no eel that she had ever seen before. Many colours danced upon the surface of its skin. 'What a strange creature you are,' she whispered, 'and what a pity it is that you cannot speak to me.'

'What is it that you want to know?' the eel enquired.

Medb was astonished that the eel could speak. 'What kind of beast are you?' she said.

'A tormented one,' the eel replied. 'I have lived in different shapes for many years and I am tired of my wanderings.' With that, it slithered out of the vessel and swam away in the water. A short time after that, it was swallowed up by a cow that came to drink at the spring.

Now the two swineherds underwent their final transformations. Rucht, who had been swallowed by Medb's cow, was reborn as the White-horned Bull, while Friuch was calved as the Brown Bull of Cooley. And in their final shapes, the quarrelling pig-keepers led all the peoples of Ulster and Connacht into war.

Once Medb had resolved to steal the Bull of Cooley, she wasted no time in mustering her forces. A great army was assembled at Cruachan and messengers were sent out to recruit allies from the other provinces. Ailill summoned his brothers, the sons of Mágach, and the exiled Ulstermen, Fergus Mac Roth and Cormac, the son of Conchobar, were also in the company.

Cormac's forces were ranged in three troops. The first troop wore fine green cloaks, with silver brooches. Their shirts were embroidered with gold and the hilts of their swords were inlaid with amber and ivory. The second troop had clipped hair and long, grey cloaks. Golden decoration glittered on their shields and their swords were made of pure white metal. Cormac himself came with the final troop, who looked resplendent in their rich purple cloaks and their crimson-hooded tunics. They had jewelled brooches at their breasts and the mighty spears that they brandished seemed as large as pillars.

This mighty host made its camp there, between the four fords of Ai, Athmaga, Athslisen and Athberena. Red fires blazed throughout the night, as the army prepared to depart. But Medb held them back for a fortnight, waiting for a sign from her druids that the omens were favourable. They could tell her nothing, except that she would return safely, whatever might befall her troops.

At the end of two weeks, the army could wait no longer and Medb gave the order to break camp. As she did so, she turned to her charioteer and said: 'Everyone who has a lover, a relative or a friend in this company will curse me today, for this host is gathered here on my account.'

Then, as her chariot was turned, Medb saw a strange thing. A young woman was sitting on the shaft of a chariot, staring at her. She had golden hair and a cloak of many colours, pinned with a golden brooch. Her skin was as pale as the snow of a single night, her teeth were like rows of pearls, her eyes had triple irises, and her voice, when she spoke, was like the gentle strumming of a harp. In her hand, she held a sword of white bronze, ringed with seven bands of gold, and she turned it around, as if she was weaving a web. Two jet-black horses were yoked to her chariot.

Medb approached her and asked, 'What is your name, young maiden?'

'I am Fedelm, the prophetess of Connacht,' she replied.

'And where have you come from?' asked Medb.

'From Scotland, where I learned to read the signs.'

'And have you truly the gift of foresight?'

'I have,' answered Fedelm.

'Then look into the future and tell me what you see for my people,' instructed Medb.

The girl obeyed and said. 'I see crimson on them, I see red.'

'That cannot be,' answered Medb, 'for Conchobar lies stricken at Emain Macha. My messengers have come from there, confirming it. We have nothing to fear from him or his Ulstermen. Look again, Fedelm. How will it really be with my people?'

'I see crimson on them, I see red,' the girl repeated.

'Impossible,' said Medb once again. 'For Celtchair, son of Uthecar, is also stricken with the weakness, and a third of the Ulstermen alongside him. My messengers have just returned from his fort, assuring me of this. And, besides, Fergus Mac Roth, the greatest of their warriors, has joined with us, bringing a force of three thousand men. You cannot be right. Look again, maiden.'

'I see crimson, I see red,' Fedelm declared once more.

Medb racked her brain for other explanations for the prediction. 'Perhaps there is nothing to fear in your vision. For, whenever any army gathers, there is bound to be a certain amount of row-diness and squabbling. Warriors may come to blows over the tiniest matters, such as who has the right to cross a ford first or who has the right to kill the first stag. Is this what you are referring to, Fedelm? Is this what you see for my forces?'

'I see crimson on them, I see red,' uttered the girl for the final time. 'I see a man, low in stature, performing great feats of arms. I see many wounds on his smooth skin, but victory on his brow. He is young, beautiful and modest towards women, but as fierce as a dragon in battle. I do not recognize him, but I know this much. He will redden the men of your army with their own blood. The dead will lie thick on the ground and he will carry away many heads with him.'

This is the prophecy that Fedelm delivered to Medb of Connacht.

Medb ordered her forces to march on Cooley. In spite of Fedelm's warnings, she felt confident that they would succeed. For she knew that the Ulstermen lay under a curse, which made them too weak to fight. This is the story of how the Ulstermen came to be afflicted.

There was in Ulster a rich landowner named Crunniuc, the son of Agnoman. He lived in a remote, mountainous part of the province together with his sons. His wife was dead and, so, he was oblig-ed to manage the running of the house himself. Then, one day, while he was sitting there alone, an unknown woman entered the place. She was tall, finely-dressed and had noble features. Crunniuc looked up at her, expecting her to say something as a greeting, but the woman just remained silent. Instead, she walked straight over to the hearth and began tending to the fire, as if she were a mere serving-maid. After she had done this, she put the household in order, prepared a meal, and went out to milk the cows. That night, she slept with Crunniuc. And, in all this time, she never uttered a word to him.

The woman stayed on at Crunniuc's house and, some time later, she married him. She contin-ued to manage his household, look after his sons and, in due course, she informed him that she was expecting their own child. All seemed well until the day of the great festival, when the men of Ulster met to compete in races, games and other amusements. Crunniuc decided to go, since all the other men of his standing were to be there, but his wife warned him against it. 'Do not go,' she pleaded, 'for if you so much as mention my name, I will be lost to you forever.'

'If that is the case, I shall take care that I do not speak of you at all,' Crunniuc assured her. So saying, he made ready then set off for the fair. The event proved to be just as grand an occasion as he had anti-cipated. The highlight occurred towards the end of the day, when the king's chariot was brought out onto the field. It won the main race with ease and the poets, the druids and the assembled crowds all joined together to praise the feat of the royal horses. 'Nothing can match the speed

CERNUNNOS

Detail from the Gundestrop Cauldron showing Cernunnos as Lord of all Animals.
He holds a torc and a ram-horned snake.

CERNUNNOS WAS a horned god, one of the most ancient Celtic deities. He is known to have predated the Roman influence in western Europe, with images from as early as the fourth century BC. In essence, he was a nature god, symbolizing fertility and plenty. He was also lord of the animals and typical representations show him squatting on the ground, surrounded by the beasts of the forest. Abundance was symbolized by sacks of money or cornucopias, which were placed in his lap, and his role as a fertility god was often emphasized by the presence of a ram-horned snake. He is portrayed in this way on the Gundestrup Cauldron. Cernunnos was usually depicted with antlers, although images with other animal horns can occasionally be found. On some shrines, the antlers were removable, indicating that the god may have been the focus of seasonal rituals, reflecting the annual growth and shedding of horns. In Irish legend, Cernunnos is associated with the father-god known as the Dagda, and there may also be links with the classical cult of Pan.

of these beasts,' they cried. 'There are no better runners in the whole of Ireland.'

Crunniuc scoffed at this. 'Why, my wife could run faster than them.' These foolish words were overheard and the king was informed. His wrath was fearsome to behold. 'Take hold of the man,' he ordered, 'and keep him prisoner until his wife is brought here. She must be willing to make good his boast.'

So, the king's men held Crunniuc fast and messengers were sent to his house, to fetch his wife. When she heard what her husband had done, she pleaded with the messengers: 'What he said was rash indeed, but I cannot come. As you can see, I am full with child and my time is near.'

'That would be a great pity,' said the men, 'for if you do not come with us, your husband will be put to death.'

'Then I have no choice,' she said. 'I must go with you, whatever happens.'

So, Crunniuc's wife accompanied the messengers to the festival, where she was brought before the king. Once more, she immediately asked for mercy, showing him her condition. She even asked for a delay, promising to race against the royal chariot team after she had given birth to her child. But the king would brook no delay, stating that her husband would forfeit his life if she refused to run straight away.

Then the woman turned to the people of Ulster, who were gathered there in their thousands. 'Help me,' she cried out. 'Surely, you must see my plight, for a mother bore each and every one of you. Help me, pity me. Wait until my child is born.' But the crowd was also unmoved and urged her to race for them.

'Very well,' she said, 'but great evil will come of this, and it will afflict the whole of Ulster.'

'What is your name?' demanded the king.

'I am Macha, daughter of Sainrith mac Imbath, and I promise you that my name and those of my heirs will mark this place forever.'

Then she went out to where the horses were waiting with the king's chariot. The race began and Macha outran the horses, beating them to the winning point. But the effort cost her greatly and there, at that very spot, the pains of childbirth came upon her. She screamed out as two children were born to her, one boy and one girl. That is why the place was later known as Emain Macha, or 'the Twins of Macha.'

In her agony, Macha placed a curse on the men of Ulster, saying that all those who heard her cries would come to know the pain she had just experienced. For five days and four nights, they would suffer the same pain and weakness as a woman giving birth. And this curse would afflict all the men of Ulster and it would also be passed down to their heirs. For nine generations, they would suffer in the same way, and the weakness would come upon them in the hour of their greatest need, when their enemies were closing in on them. Only three classes of people were spared from this debilitating fate. They were all the young boys of Ulster, the women of Ulster and the family of Cú Chulainn.

This is the dreadful weakness that afflicted the men of Ulster, when Medb and Ailill moved their armies against them.

CÚ CHULAINN'S PROWESS

T LAST, IT WAS TIME for the men of Connacht to leave Cruachan and begin their march towards Cooley. The first day brought them as far as Cuilsilinne, and they made their camp there for the night. In the evening, Medb consulted with her chiefs as to who should lead the army in their march. Between them, they decided that Fergus would be the best choice, since he was an exile from Ulster and knew the territory.

So, Fergus was given command of the army and, on the following day, he led them out of Cuilsilinne. But, although he had become estranged from Conchobar, Fergus retained a deep affection for his native province. Because of this, he sent word to the men of Ulster, warning them of the force that was coming their way. In addition, he tried to give them time to muster their defences, by taking Medb's people on an elaborate detour. He led them through bogs and streams, taking them first south and then north, so that at the end of the day they were exhausted, even though they had only advanced a short way.

Soon, however, Medb and Ailill became suspicious. They challenged Fergus, accusing him of treachery, for letting his old friendship for Ulster sway his actions. Fergus denied this hotly, explaining that he had chosen this meandering route, in order to avoid crossing the path of the Hound of Culann. Secretly, though, he realized that he had been discovered, and he resolved to deceive Medb no more.

Meanwhile, Fergus's warning had reached the ears of Cú Chulainn and his father, Sualtam. Alone among the Ulstermen, they were free of the terrible weakness inflicted by Macha. They now rode out towards the border of the province, arriving at the pillar-stone of Ardcullin. There, they allowed their horses to graze. Sualtam's horse cropped the grass to its roots, while Cú Chulainn's cropped it right down to the bare flags of the pillar.

'I can sense that the armies of Connacht are not far away,' Cú Chulainn said to his father. 'You must ride back and warn the Ulstermen. Tell them not to stay out in the open plains, but to seek shelter in wooded places. I have promised to meet with a serving-maid of Fedelm Noichride tonight, but I will return to this place tomorrow and keep watch on the enemy's progress.'

Sualtam was concerned that the border was to be deserted that night, but he did as his son requested. Cú Chulainn, too, regretted having given his word to the young woman. So, before he left, he took a sapling from the forest nearby, bent it into a hoop with one hand, and carved a message in Ogham upon it. Then he wedged the hoop around the pillar-stone and went off to keep his assignation.

A short time later, a scouting party from the Connacht army came upon the pillar-stone. These were the four sons of Iraird mac Anchinne, Eirr and Indell, and their charioteers Foich and Fochlam. They noticed the signs of grazing around the marker and the hoop with the Ogham message. They took the latter and showed it to Fergus. Immediately, he called the troops to a halt.

Medb rode up to Fergus and demanded to know why they had stopped. Privately, she thought it might be yet another of his diversions. He, however, showed her the message on the hoop. This bore Cú Chulainn's name and a warning, which read: 'Go no further, unless you have a man amongst you who can make a hoop like this, using just one hand. My friend Fergus is excluded from this test.'

Medb passed the hoop to her druids for them to look at it. They confirmed that there was a *geis* or taboo upon it; if it was ignored, the carver of the message would inflict great harm on them. 'It would be a shame if our side were to bear the first losses in this undertaking,' said Ailill. 'Let us make our way, instead, through that forest to the south. Then we will not have to pass by the pillar-stone at all.'

This plan was approved and the warriors of Connacht proceeded to cut a path through the forest, so that their chariots could drive straight through it. And, from that time on, the place was known as Slechta or 'the Cut Way'. They camped there that evening and, during the night, a great snow fell, turning all the provinces of Ireland into a single, frosted plain. Next morning, they arose early and advanced into the Ulstermen's territory.

Cú Chulainn, on the other hand, was late in rising. The serving-girl made him food and brought him pure water, so that he could bathe. Then he ordered his charioteer, Laeg, to prepare the horses and they set out towards the border. After a while, they saw the tracks made by the Connacht army and realized that it had crossed into Ulster. Bitterly, Cú Chulainn lamented his meeting with the girl. 'I wish that I had not gone there,' he moaned, 'for now an army has passed unannounced into Ulster.'

So, stricken with remorse, he urged his chariot on, desperate to confront the foe. His wish was soon granted. For, at a place called Athgowla, north of Knowth, he came upon the four sons of Iraird mac Anchinne. Swiftly, he killed them, severing their heads from their bodies. Then he cut down a tree with a single stroke of his sword, lopped off all but four branches, and rammed the trunk into the bed of

43

a nearby stream. On the tips of these four branches, he impaled the heads of his victims. Next, he turned their chariots around and whipped the horses, so that they would carry the evidence of his deed back to Medb and her forces.

Sure enough, the blood-smeared chariots thundered back to Medb and her people. And there, the sight was greeted with alarm, for it seemed certain that some part of the army of Ulster must be lying in wait for them nearby. When they followed the tracks back to the stream, however, and saw the four impaled heads still dripping with gore, they noticed only a single chariot track; and it was clear that the tree had been felled with a single sword-stroke.

'Can one man alone have done all this?' asked Ailill.

'Indeed, he can,' replied Fergus. And that night, when the people of Connacht had made their camp and taken their fill of food, he told them of Cú Chulainn and of the marvellous feats that he had achieved in his brief life. In this way, the men of Connacht came to learn of the awesome prowess of the enemy that they were about to confront.

While the forces of Connacht continued their search for the bull, Cú Chulainn harried them, hoping to delay them long enough for his fellow-countrymen to recover from their weakness. He killed valiant Fraech in the river at Ath Fuait; he slew the six Dungals of Irress at Ath Taiten; and he killed Orlam, forcing his charioteer to carry the head back, to show the men of Connacht. Cú Chulainn even made direct attempts on the life of Medb. With his sling, he killed a squirrel that had climbed on her shoulder, and also a waiting-woman that he mistook for her. Soon, he engendered such fear that no man wished to venture away from the main body of the army, while Medb herself was constantly accompanied by men with shields, protecting her from the Hound of Ulster's slingshots. It was even said that, on one night alone, a hundred men died of fright after hearing the sound of Cú Chulainn's weapons.

The carnage increased further, when the army reached Druim Feine in Conaille. There, Cú Chulainn harassed them from a distance with his sling. From his vantage point at Ochaine, he killed a hundred men on each of the three nights that the invaders rested there.

'This is hopeless,' cried Ailill. 'Our army will disappear, if we do not stem this flow of blood. Let us make a pact with him. I will offer him a portion of the plain of Ai that is equal in size to the whole of Muirthemne. In addition, he may have my finest chariot, harnessed and equipped with a dozen men. Or, if he prefers it, he may have the plain where he was raised, along with full compensation for all the cattle and household goods that we have destroyed. All he has to do in exchange is to swear his full allegiance to me; a small enough thing to ask, since I am a far superior master to that half-king, Conchobar.'

So Fergus Mac Roth – the herald, who could circle the whole of Ireland in just one day – was sent to bear this message to Cú Chulainn. He found the boy warrior at Delga, resting after his labours.

'I see a man coming towards us,' said Laeg, turning to Cú Chulainn.

'Then describe him, charioteer,' instructed Cú Chulainn.

'He has a full head of yellow hair, wrapped around with a linen band; he wears a hooded tunic and a brown cloak, fastened with a spear-shaped brooch; he carries a white hazel rod in one hand and a vicious-looking club in the other; and at his waist is a sword with a sea-horse tooth for a hilt,' replied Laeg.

'Let him come,' said Cú Chulainn, 'for these are the tokens of a herald.'

Mac Roth approached and asked the young warrior for his name.

'I am a servant of Conchobar Mac Nessa,' Cú Chulainn replied.

NEWGRANGE

THE INTRICATELY decorated passage-grave at Newgrange is arguably the most impressive monument of its kind in Europe. Situated 32 km (20 miles) out of Dublin, it dates back to around 3000 BC and forms part of a larger megalithic site called the Brugh na Bóinne. This includes two other tumuli, Knowth and Dowth, and a number of standing stones. Newgrange is particularly famous for its elaborate carvings, both inside and outside the tomb. These consist mainly of abstract patterns – such as spirals, chevrons and lozenges – and although they were created many centuries before the arrival of the Celts, they exerted a profound influence on the craftsmen of the La Tène period. The original architects of Newgrange aligned the tomb with the winter solstice in order that, at sunrise on 21 December, a shaft of light penetrates through a small aperture and lights up the interior of the chamber, just reaching a stone basin that once contained the cremated remains of the dead.

It is not known whether the Celts used Newgrange for any ritual purpose, but it was clearly important to them. It is mentioned many times in their early tales and the name of the tomb means 'the cave of Gráinne', a reference to a leading character in the Fionn Cycle.

'Is that the best answer you can give me?' asked Mac Roth.

'It will suffice,' replied Cú Chulainn.

'Can you tell me, then, where I might find Cú Chulainn?' continued Mac Roth.

'What would you say to him, if he was here?' asked Cú Chulainn. When he heard this, Mac Roth guessed that this imperious young man was Cú Chulainn himself and he delivered his message. But the youth continued to talk in the most disdainful manner.

'If Cú Chulainn were here', he said disdainfully, 'he would reject your offer. He would not trade his mother's brother for another king.'

So Mac Roth went back to his masters, and returned a short time later with a new message. Ailill now offered Cú Chulainn all the noblest women and the cows without milk from the booty they had plundered. All that was asked in return, was that he should stop attacking them with his sling by night, though he could do as he wished during the day.

Cú Chulainn was as scornful as before. 'I will not agree to that. For, if you take away our serving-women, our noble ladies will be forced to do menial work, and without milch-cows we will have no milk.'

Once more, Mac Roth departed, to obtain new conditions, which were soon forthcoming. Ailill now promised Cú Chulainn all the serving-women and the milch-cows that they had seized. Still, however, the youth was not satisfied. 'I cannot agree to that,' he replied, 'for then the Ulstermen would take serving-women to their beds and would breed a race of slaves. Besides that, they would have to use the milch-cows for meat in the winter.'

'Are there any terms which would satisfy you?' the herald then enquired.

'There are,' replied Cú Chulainn, 'but you must find them out for yourself. One man in the Connacht camp will know exactly what I mean. If you send him to me with the offer, I promise that I will accept it.'

Mac Roth returned to his masters with this puzzling answer. They did not know what to make of it, until Fergus provided the explanation. 'I know what he has in mind,' he said, 'though it is scarcely good news for you. He will fight the men of Connacht one by one, at the ford. While the combat is in progress, your army may march on unhindered. But, as soon as he has defeated the man sent against him, it must stop and make camp until the following day. In this way, he means to delay you until the men of Ulster have recovered from their weakness.'

'Even so,' said Ailill, 'it will be far better for us to lose a single man every day, rather than a hundred every night. Go to him, Fergus, and tell him we accept his offer.'

As Fergus set out on his mission, he was followed by Etarcomol, a foster-son of Medb and Ailill.

'I would rather that you did not accompany me,' said Fergus, 'not out of any personal dislike, but because I think your pride and insolence will lead you into trouble.'

'Could you not place me under your protection then?' said Etarcomol.

'I could,' answered Fergus, 'provided that you treat Cú Chulainn with respect.'

The young man agreed and, so, the two of them rode in their chariots to Delga. There, Cú

Chulainn greeted Fergus with delight. 'Welcome, dear friend,' he cried. 'If there was salmon in the estuary, I'd give you one and share another; if a flock of birds alighted on the plain, I'd give you one and share another; I'd offer you the three herbs of friendship – watercress, marshwort and sea-weed; I'd bring you a drink from the sands, cupped in my hands; and, if there was a combat at the ford, I would fight in your place, so that you might sleep.'

'I believe it,' said Fergus with a smile, ' but I have not come here to test your generosity. I know you have little enough food as it is.' With this, he repeated the words of Ailill and the pact was made between them. Then, after a further exchange of compliments, he turned his chariot around and began the journey back.

But Etarcomol lingered for a moment, however, staring very hard at Cú Chulainn. 'What are you gawping at?' the latter asked.

'You,' came the reply.

'That shouldn't take long', retorted Cú Chulainn.

'Precisely,' replied Etarcomol. 'I cannot see why such a fuss is made of you. I can see no cause for panic or terror. I see only a fine-looking boy, who would be better off playing children's games with wooden weapons.'

'You insult me,' said Cú Chulainn, 'but for Fergus's sake, I will spare you. If it was not for his protection, I would have run you through by now and scattered your entrails all around this field.'

'There's no need to threaten me,' said Etarcomol, 'Now that you have made your pact with Ailill, I will take the earliest opportunity of meeting you in single combat. Expect to see me at the ford tomorrow.' With that, he swung his chariot around and headed after Fergus. He did not go far, however, before his impatience got the better of him. Turning to his charioteer, he cried: 'I have sworn to fight Cú Chulainn tomorrow, but I cannot wait that long. Bring the horses around and I will face him now.' Cú Chulainn looked grim, as Etarcomol drew near him again. 'I have told you that I do not wish to fight you,' he said forcefully.

'You have no choice in the matter,' replied the other, launching his first attack. But Cú Chulainn just swayed out of the way and, with a scything stroke from his sword, he cut the earth from beneath his opponent's feet, so that Etarcomol fell hard on his back.

'Get away from me, you fool,' said Cú Chulainn. 'I have no wish to spill your blood. If I had, I'd have cut you to ribbons by now.'

Etarcomol leaped to his feet, furious at the indignity

47

he had suffered. 'No!' he shouted, 'I won't leave here, unless I carry your head away with me.'

Still, Cú Chulainn remained patient. He lunged twice with his sword, just below his enemy's armpits. The blows caused Etarcomol's clothing to fall at his feet, but did not so much as scratch his skin. Then, when this failed to discourage the man, Cú Chulainn struck again. This time, his blade sheared through the hair on his head, as sharp as any razor, and once again not a drop of blood was spilled. But Etarcomol was persistent and, now, Cú Chulainn's patience was at an end. With a mighty swing, he brought his sword right down through the man's skull and split him apart right down to his navel.

It was not long before Fergus realized that something was wrong. His worst fears were confirmed, when he saw Etarcomol's chariot heading towards him with just the driver inside. Angrily, he turned back to complain to Cú Chulainn.

'You have shamed me, lad,' he called out. 'That fellow was under my protection.'

'Don't be angry, Fergus,' said Cú Chulainn meekly. 'I was not to blame for the fight. Ask Etarcomol's charioteer.'

'What you say is true,' confirmed the latter, and proceeded to tell Fergus the whole story.

'He boasted that he would carry away my head,' added Cú Chulainn. 'What do you think I should have done?'

Fergus had no hesitation in answering. 'You did the right thing,' he replied. 'The man was an arrogant fool.' So saying, he hobbled Etarcomol's legs and attached them to the back of his chariot. Then he dragged the corpse back to the Connacht camp. It became so badly mangled in the

process, that it almost fell apart when the chariot went over rough ground.

Medb was most displeased, when she saw one of her men returning in this fashion. 'That is no way to treat a courageous warrior,' she called out.

'He deserved it,' growled Fergus. 'He should not have picked a fight with the Hound of Culann.'

So they dug a grave for Etarcomol and grieved for him. A stone was placed on top, and his name was scratched on it in Ogham letters.

True to his word, Cú Chulainn put his sling away and killed no Connacht men that night.

Medb took a third of her forces and made a sortie into the district of Cuib, hunting for the Bull. Cú Chulainn tried to follow her but, on the road to Midluachair, he came across something unexpected. It was a powerful-looking stranger, driving a bull and fifteen heifers, and he was accompanied by three score of Ailill's men. They had their cloaks fastened tight about them, so that they would not be recognized. Even so, Cú Chulainn was suspicious.

'Where have you come from with those cattle?' he cried out.

'From that mountain over there,' the man replied.

'And where are their cowherds?'

'I am the only one,' said the stranger, hurrying on his way.

Cú Chulainn did not care for this answer and followed the man as far as the ford.

'What is your name?' he called out.

'One who neither fears nor loves you. My name is Bude Mac Bain.'

'Then here's my javelin for you, Bude,' said Cú Chulainn, and he hurled it at the man, striking him below the rib-cage and piercing his liver. The fellow dropped dead instantly and the ford is now named Ath Bude, in memory of this feat of arms. Cú Chulainn hastened towards the other warriors but, in the ensuing mêlée, the Bull was driven off and taken into Medb's camp.

As Cú Chulainn lay sleeping one night, a terrible cry awoke him from his slumbers. Rising up, he saw Laeg yoking the horses to his chariot. 'The noise came from that direction,' he said, pointing to the north.

'Very well, let us see if we can find out what caused it,' said Cú Chulainn, mounting the chariot. They drove in the darkness for a short time, until they came across a young woman, who seemed to be waiting for them. Her appearance was very striking. She wore a long, red dress and a crimson cloak that trailed on the ground behind her. The horses that pulled her chariot were also red.

'Who are you?' enquired Cú Chulainn.

'I am King Buan's daughter,' was the reply, 'and I have come in search of you. I have heard wondrous tales of your strength and bravery, and I offer you both my love and my treasure.'

'You have chosen a bad time for this,' said Cú Chulainn, 'for the hardships of war have made me tired and famished. I am in no position to deal nicely with a woman.'

'But I will help you,' said the woman. 'I will do everything in my power to protect you ...'

Cú Chulainn cut her short. 'I do not need the protection of a woman.'

'In that case, I will hinder you,' she said, her tone changing ominously. 'When warriors come against you in the ford, I will turn into an eel at your feet and trip you up.'

'That sounds more feasible than your tale about being the daughter of a king. In any case, if I catch you, I'll crack your ribs between my toes and you'll carry that wound forever, unless I heal you myself,' replied Cú Chulainn.

'Then I will turn into a grey she-wolf and send cattle stampeding towards you,' said the woman.

'And I'll hurl a stone from my sling and burst one of your eyes, and you'll carry that wound forever, unless I heal you myself,' exclaimed Cú Chulainn.

'Then I'll become a hornless red heifer and trample you under my feet,' retorted the woman.

'Before you manage that, I'll hurl another stone and shatter your legs beneath you. And you'll remain crippled in that way forever, unless I heal you myself,' were Cú Chulainn's final words.

Having spoken thus, Cú Chulainn made a move towards the woman. But, in a moment, she and her chariot were gone. All that remained was a black crow, sitting on the branch of a tree. From this, Cú Chulainn knew that he had been talking with the war goddess, the Morrigán.

MORRIGAN

THE MORRIGÁN WAS the supreme Celtic war goddess, hovering over battlefields to incite soldiers and scavenge upon the dead. She plays a crucial role in the tale of Cú Chulainn. At first, she attempts to woo him but, once rejected, she becomes an implacable enemy, determined to bring about his doom. She has the power of prophecy and is also a shapeshifter, usually assuming the form of a crow or raven. It has been suggested that she may be the forerunner of Morgan Le Fay in the Arthurian cycle. The Morrigán was a threefold goddess and she figures in the Irish legends either in her own guise or in one of her subsidiary aspects —

as Badb, Macha or Nemain. These characters are more or less interchangeable, although they feature in different legends. Macha placed a curse upon the men of Ulster, after being forced to race against the king's horses whilst pregnant; Nemain's terrible howl caused a hundred warriors to die of fright; and Badb was often seen at a ford before a battle, cleansing the weapons of soldiers who were about to die. The Morrigán allied her destructive nature with an intense, sexual potency; the combined associations of fertility and death link the goddess with the Sheela-na-gig, a grotesque figure carved on many Irish churches and castles.

VALOUR AT THE FORD

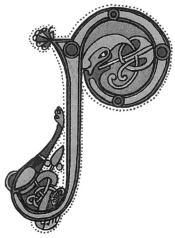

RESENTLY, LOCH MAC Emonis came to challenge Cú Chulainn at the ford. He was offered a fine reward for meeting the Ulsterman, namely a wide stretch of land on the plain of Ai and a war chariot equipped with a dozen men. But Loch thought it was beneath his dignity to cross swords with a mere stripling and, so, he sent his brother Long to fight in his place.

Cú Chulainn soon made short work of Long Mac Emonis and the headless body was carried back from the ford to Loch, to shame him into avenging his brother's death. Still, however, Loch refused to fight with a beardless boy. So the women of Connacht called out to Cú Chulainn, saying that all his victories were nothing, because none of their best warriors would pit their strength against a smooth-skinned youth. These words really stung Cú Chulainn. He plucked a handful of grass and said a spell over it, so that everyone would think this was his beard. The ruse worked. The women of Connacht reported back to Loch that the Ulsterman was bearded and, at last, he consented to meet with him.

Their combat took place a little way upstream, since Loch did not wish to fight at the spot where his brother had died. The initial exchanges were fierce, as both men matched each other blow for blow. Then Cú Chulainn felt something tugging at his feet. A huge, black eel coiled three times around his ankle and sent him tumbling into the water. While he lay there, Loch flailed at him with his sword, turning the shallows red with Cú Chulainn's blood.

Fergus was watching from the bank and he urged his followers to taunt Cú Chulainn, to goad him into fighting back. Venom-tongued Bricriu was happy to oblige. 'Are you going to be beaten by a little fish,' he cried out. 'You should never have appointed yourself as champion if that's the best you can do, with all the men of Ireland looking on.'

Spurred on by this, Cú Chulainn clambered up, dashing the eel against a stone, so that its ribs were broken. The creature loosened its grip but, almost at once, it turned into a grey she-wolf and brought cattle stampeding against him. Undaunted, Cú Chulainn took out his sling and sent a sharp stone speeding into the eye of the wolf. It reeled back in pain, just as Loch's sword cut into the Ulsterman once again.

Now the Morrigán came at Cú Chulainn in her final form, a hornless red heifer hurtling towards him. But the Hound of Ulster aimed his sling once more, loosing a shot that broke the animal's legs beneath her. The Morrigán came at him no more and so, finally, Cú Chulainn turned his full attention upon Loch. His wounds were beginning to hurt him, so he ended the duel quickly by taking up his trusty spear, the fearsome Gae Bolga. With all his remaining strength, he sent it skimming over the waters into Loch's stomach. There, the barbs opened out and shredded the man's guts. Loch collapsed back dead in the water.

Then Cú Chulainn walked over to his fallen foe and cut his head off.

After his battle with Loch Mac Emonis, Cú Chulainn felt a great weariness come over him. And, as he walked away from the ford, nursing his bleeding wounds, he encountered a crippled, one-eyed hag milking a cow. It was a strange cow, for it had only three teats, but Cú Chulainn thought nothing of this. All he knew was that he felt an overwhelming tiredness from his battles and a burning thirst.

So he approached the old hag and asked her for a drink of milk from one of the teats. She agreed to this and gave him the milk. Instantly, he felt much refreshed. 'Good health to you for

SHAPE-SHIFTERS

Silver coin, third century BC. It was thought that many gods could assume the shape of a boar, which was also a potent war symbol.

MAGIC AND THE supernatural play a major role in early Celtic literature, moulding the destinies of all the leading characters. Shape-shifting, along with prophecies and curses, was the most commonplace of these magical interventions. The gods could assume a variety of guises and, in many cases, were capable of inflicting similar changes upon mortals. Often, the transformations involved animals, although other variations were possible. In the *Mabinogion*, for example, Pwyll takes on the form and identity of a lord of the Otherworld. The Celts also had a fondness for multiple changes. For example, in the Scottish ballad of Tam Lin, Janet can only rescue her lover from the fairy throng if she holds onto him as he goes through a series of perilous transformations. Among other things, the hero turns into a snake, a toad, a swan and then a red-hot iron rod. Significantly, Tam Lin's salvation can only be attained during the festival of Samhain (Hallowe'en), as this is the period when the boundaries between the real and the supernatural worlds are broken down, and strange transformations are most likely to occur.

The Celts' fascination with shape-shifting was reflected in their imaginative artworks. In fields such as metalwork and manuscript illumination, craftsmen loved using designs that appeared abstract at first glance but which, on closer examination, conjured up the appearance of an animal's head or body.

your gift,' he said to the hag. And, as he spoke these words, the woman straightened herself up a little on her stool.

Then the hag gave him a drink from the second teat. It tasted as good as before and Cú Chulainn thanked her again, saying: 'Good health to you for your gift.' With this, the woman stretched out her leg and he could see that she was no longer lame.

Now the hag offered him a drink from the final teat. Cú Chulainn took it greedily, feeling the energy return to his body. 'Good health to you for your gift,' he said once more. And, after these words, the woman turned to look at him, and he could see that her blind eye had been made well. On her face, there was a smile that was all too familiar.

'You said that you would never heal me,' said the Morrígán.

'If I had known it was you, I would never have done so,' replied Cú Chulainn bitterly.

That night, while Cú Chulainn lay resting, Laeg stood watch. And he saw a man approaching them from the northeast, walking straight through the camp of the Connacht army. There was something unworldly in his bearing, so he immediately alerted Cú Chulainn.

'There is a lone man coming towards us, little Hound,' he said.

'Describe him, charioteer,' replied Cú Chulainn.

'He is fair and tall and shining. He wears a green mantle, fastened at his breast with a silver brooch. His tunic is of royal silk, and he carries a black shield and a spear with five prongs. But, the strange thing is, he is brandishing his weapons vigorously, and yet no one comes to challenge or attack him. It is as if nobody can see him.'

'You're quite right,' said Cú Chulainn. 'Nobody can see him, for that must be one of my friends from the sidhe, the fairy dwelling places, who has come to aid me in my time of need.'

This proved to be true for, when the stranger drew near, he stooped over the stricken hero and spoke sympathetically, 'You have fought manfully, Cú Chulainn, and now it is my turn to help you.'

'Who are you?' asked Cú Chulainn.

'I am Lugh, your father from the sidhe and I have come to heal your wounds. Sleep now, and I will stand watch in your place.'

So Cú Chulainn slept continuously for three days and three nights at the grave-mound of Lerga. None of the sounds of war could wake him, for he had not slept properly for months; not from the Monday after the feast of Samhain until the Wednesday after the feast of Imbolc. In all this time, he had only enjoyed brief moments of sleep at midday, when he rested his head on his spear. Otherwise, every hour of the day was spent in cutting and slashing and killing the forces that were gathered against Ulster.

While Cú Chulainn slept, Lugh placed the herbs of curing and the charms of healing on his wounds. In this way, he recovered his strength without knowing it. When he awoke at the end of three days, he felt fit enough for anything; from fighting to feasting, from carousing to love-making.

'How long have I been asleep?' he asked.

'Three days and three nights,' was Lugh's reply.

'That is bad news indeed,' Cú Chulainn said, 'for it must mean that no one has harried Medb's armies in all that time.'

Cú Chulainn was then told that, while he was asleep, the boy troop of Ulster had fought in his place. They, like him, were exempt from Macha's curse. In their three attacks, they had managed to kill three times their own number, but in doing so all of them had been slain.

When he heard this news Cú Chulainn was filled with a terrible anger and a longing for revenge. He ordered Laeg to yoke up his sickle-chariot, while he donned a marvellous array of armour. He put on twenty-seven waxed skin tunics, fastened with cords so that they wouldn't burst apart when the warp-spasm came upon him. Over these, he wore his battle-girdle of tanned leather, which was tough enough to repel the point of any spear or sword. Then he fitted iron armour-plate onto his horses, adding spikes and spear-points to every joint, so that they would slice the skin of any warrior who came near. He also cast a spell of covering over the horses and his charioteer, making them all but invisible to his enemies. Next, he took up the arms that he would use that day – his ivory-hilted sword, his eight short swords, his five-pronged spear, his eight javelins, his eight darts and his shield with the razor-sharp edge. Then he donned his crested war-helmet. This had been cunningly crafted, so that his every shout was magnified and distorted, giving the impression that goblins and fiends were fighting at his shoulder. Last of all, he drew a cloak of concealment about him, a present from Lugh, which was made out of cloth from the Land of Promise.

When all was ready, Cú Chulainn felt the warp-spasm come upon him. His features, his joints, his limbs, all were contorted until he became a hideous, shapeless thing. His entire body quivered violently, like a willow bough in a gale or a reed caught in a torrent. Fury tightened his nerves and sinews into knots and shifted them around his torso. The veins in his temple were now in his neck, while his calves and his shins were tugged round to the back of his legs. His face turned into a sickening mask of red, throbbing flesh. One eye was drawn so far back inside the skull that a wild crane could have flown into the hollow and hidden there, while the other dangled on his cheek like a soft fruit. His cheeks peeled back from his jawbone until his gullet was exposed, and his lungs and liver rose to his throat. Cú Chulainn's hair curled snake-like on his head and, above it, the air turned to a boiling mist with the heat of his rage. A light shone out from his forehead, bright as a halo, and sprays of smoke-black blood spurted from the top of his skull.

With all these contortions running through him, Cú Chulainn leaped into his chariot and thundered towards his enemy. He killed a hundred men in his first attack and then drove his horses furiously, to make a circuit around the remainder. The iron wheels of his chariot formed deep trenches, so that none of them should escape until he had wreaked his vengeance for the boy troop of Ulster. He circled around the army three times, hacking furiously with his sword until dead bodies lay thick on the ground. At the end of the day, less than one in three of the enemy escaped without a broken limb, a sightless eye or a lasting scar. Cú Chulainn, by contrast, retired from the fighting without a mark upon him.

After this savage onslaught, there were few volunteers left to challenge Cú Chulainn at the ford. Medb cajoled them, but the answer was always the same: 'It is not my family's turn to provide a scapegoat and, even if it were, why should I be the one?'

At length, she turned to Fergus and tried to persuade him to fight with Cú Chulainn. He refused stubbornly, arguing that he should never be expected to go into combat against a boy who was both his foster-son and his pupil. Medb was persistent, however, plying him with wine to weaken his resistance. Eventually, when he was thoroughly drunk, Fergus gave in to her entreaties and agreed to go.

The encounter took place on the following day. By this time, Fergus had devised a means of allaying his conscience. As he marched resolutely towards the ford, Cú Chulainn noticed that his scabbard was empty.

'You are a brave man, Fergus, to come against me without a sword,' said Cú Chulainn.

'It makes no difference; I would never use one on you. Instead, I would ask you to yield to me now, and I will return the favour at another time,' replied Fergus.

'You will yield to me, when I ask you?'

'That is so,' said Fergus.

So Cú Chulainn yielded before Fergus, retreating as far as Grellach Doluid, knowing that his foster-father would also yield to him on the day of the great battle.

The next man chosen to confront Cú Chulainn was Ferdia, son of Daire, the horn-skinned champion from Irrus Domnand. It was thought that he would provide a searching test of the Ulsterman's skills, since both men employed similar methods of fighting and both had been trained under the fearsome Scáthach. Indeed, the only difference between the two of them was that Ferdia did not have a spear that could match the Gae Bolga.

Now that the decision had been made, Medb sent her messengers to fetch Ferdia. At first, he refused to come, as he guessed her intentions and had no desire to fight his old companion. Medb sent some poets and satirists to mock him, knowing full well that the threat to his reputation would

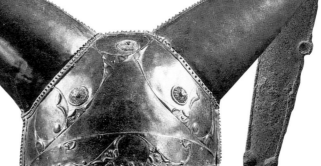

force him to change his mind. When Ferdia eventually arrived at Medb's tent, he was received with great honour and attention. Food and drink were placed before him and Findabair, Medb's daughter, sat by his side, dancing attendance upon him. She made sure that his wine goblet was always full, kissing him each time he drained it, and it was she who fed him apples and other dainties from her own fair hands.

Then, when Ferdia was relaxed and merry, Medb began to shower him with gifts. The first offering that she gave him was a magnificent chariot worth thrice seven serving-maids; the second gift was a fine stretch of arable land on the plain of Ai; the third was Medb's own leaf-shaped brooch, made of burnished gold; for the fourth gift, she pledged the hospitality of Cruachan, both for Ferdia and his descendants; and finally, best of all, she promised him the hand of her fair daughter, Findabair.

Ferdia's wits, however, were not as clouded as Medb might have hoped. 'These are wondrous gifts that you offer me,' he said to her, 'but I would sooner leave them all behind than go into battle with my foster-brother, Cú Chulainn.'

But Medb was undaunted and said: 'It is true, then, what Cú Chulainn says; that he would deem it no great triumph to conquer you.'

Ferdia was stung. 'He should never have said that. He knows full well that I would never sheathe my sword out of cowardice or fear of defeat. If he believes otherwise, he will find out differently when I meet him at the ford tomorrow.' And so, the matter was decided.

Fergus had witnessed these dealings and returned to his tent with a heavy heart. 'Alas,' he said to his followers, 'I fear that a woeful deed will be done tomorrow. My foster-son Cú Chulainn will meet his end at the ford.'

'Never! Who claims that?' they asked.

'Why, his old companion, Ferdia,' replied Fergus. 'Will one of you not ride out now and urge Cú Chulainn to leave the ford by morning?'

None of them were willing to do this, however, so Fergus gave orders for his own chariot to be harnessed and, within the hour, he was at Cú Chulainn's side. The boy warrior welcomed him openly and was eager to hear all about the purpose of his visit.

'I am here to warn you of the warrior, who will come against you at the ford tomorrow,' said Fergus.

'Let us hear who it is, then,' replied Cú Chulainn.

'It is none other than your old school-fellow, Ferdia, son of Dáire,' Fergus answered.

'With all my heart,' said Cú Chulainn, 'I wish it could be anyone other than he. Not because I fear him, but because I have such a great affection for him.'

'You would do well to have some fear of him, my foster-son, for he is a formidable warrior,' said Fergus wryly. 'He also wears a coat of horn-skinned armour that is so tough, that no sword-edge or spear-point can pierce it.'

'Say no more about it,' answered Cú Chulainn. 'I thank you for your warning, but it would not worry me if the whole host of Medb's army came against me. Combat with a single warrior, however valiant, holds no terrors. If Ferdia challenges me tomorrow, I will brush him aside, as if his limbs were nothing more than fragile reeds.'

On hearing this, Fergus left and returned to his tent. After his departure, Laeg turned to Cú Chulainn and asked him what he planned to do that night. The lad had no answer to this, so the charioteer made his point. 'Tomorrow, Ferdia will arrive at the place of combat bathed and refreshed, with his hair newly trimmed and plaited. It would please me greatly if you would go to a place, where you might receive the same treatment. Why do you not go and see your wife, Emer, at the Meadow of the Two Oxen in Slieve Fuad?'

EPONA

EPONA WAS AN ancient horse goddess whose name survives today in our word 'pony'. Uniquely for a Celtic deity, she was also worshipped by the Romans and a festival was held in her honour on 18 December. On this day, all beasts of burden were rested. The classical connection probably accounts for the unusually consistent iconography of the goddess. She was normally portrayed sitting side-saddle on a mare or standing between a group of horses.

Her symbolic role was more complex. As a mother-goddess, Epona was associated with fertility and was sometimes shown with a suckling foal. She was also linked with healing and the protection of the human soul. Common attributes included a napkin that was used to start horse races — and also, by inference, the race of life — and a large key. The latter opened the gates to the Otherworld, where Epona conducted the soul after death.

Cú Chulainn thought this very sound advice and obeyed it forthwith.

The mood in Ferdia's tent that night was much gloomier. It weighed heavily with his followers that their lord was to meet the Hound of Culann on the morrow. For was he not already the cause of sore depletions in Medb's army? Ferdia, too, was troubled. He wondered how long he was going to be able to keep the riches and the princess that had so recently been bestowed upon him. Indeed, the same might be said for his very life. For who could be sure of keeping their head on their shoulders, when they came up against Cú Chulainn in combat?

Ferdia slept little that night and rose early in the morning. He ordered his boy to yoke up his chariot and travelled to the ford shortly after daybreak.

'Look, my lad,' he said. 'Do you see Cú Chulainn at the place of combat?'

'No, he is not here,' was the reply.

'Are you sure? Look again,' said Ferdia.

'Cú Chulainn is not such a tiny speck that I wouldn't notice him if he was here,' said the charioteer sarcastically.

'Maybe he has fled. Perhaps he heard that a warrior of true mettle was coming, a different proposition to all the others that he has faced, and he decided to abandon the ford,' mused Ferdia.

The charioteer was sceptical. 'It may not be such a good idea to slander Cú Chulainn in his absence, my lord. Do you remember what happened when you lost your sword, giving battle by the Tyrrhene Sea? How it was Cú Chulainn who slew a hundred warriors to retrieve it for you? And do you not recall what happened that same night?'

'I do not,' replied Ferdia.

'We were staying at the house of Scáthach's steward and the churl fetched you a vicious blow in the small of your back with his flesh-hook. And, while you were still dazed, Cú Chulainn cut the fellow in two with his sword. You certainly would not have boasted that day that you were the better warrior.'

'You should have reminded me of all this earlier, charioteer. I might have considered longer before accepting Medb's offer. But, as we are here, spread out some skins on my chariot so that I may rest. For I slept very little this past night.'

'I will my lord, although it seems a poor place to choose. You might just as well sleep in the path of a boar hunt. But try and rest, and I will keep watch for you. You will have full warning of his arrival, unless he appears out of the mists or the clouds.' So, Ferdia lay down and rested on the chariot, but sleep would not come to him.

It was not long after this, that the charioteer laid his arm gently on his master's shoulder. Ferdia rose up and watched as Cú Chulainn approached, his horses sweeping across the countryside like the gusting of a spring wind or the flight of a stag set upon by hounds.

Ferdia greeted Cú Chulainn and the pair reminisced about their youthful friendship, during the time they spent with Scáthach. There were many reproaches, as each tried to persuade the other to leave the ford. At last, they accepted that they had to fight and Ferdia offered Cú Chulainn the choice of weapons.

Cú Chulainn declined. 'No,' he said. 'You arrived at the ford first. You have the right to choose.'
So Ferdia made the first choice, opting for the casting weapons that they had used so often on Scáthach's practice field. Swiftly, they assembled these – the round-handled spears, the quill darts,

the ivory-hilted daggers — and began hurling them at one another. All morning, the missiles were thrown from one against the other, making a sound like bees in flight. But both warriors were so skilled at fending the spears off with their shields that no harm was done. At midday, they agreed to stop, since their weapons were all blunted, and they handed the broken darts and spears to their charioteers. In the afternoon, they switched to their broad spears, bound with flaxen cord. For several hours, they hurled these at each other until both men were exhausted.

'Let us leave this now,' said Ferdia, as nightfall approached. 'Agreed,' said Cú Chulainn. 'The time is right to stop.'

So they left off fighting, cast their spears away and embraced each other warmly. Their horses were put in the one enclosure that night and their charioteers shared the same fire. Green rushes were laid out for them and healers came to dress their wounds. And Cú Chulainn made sure that for every plant and herb that was placed on one of his cuts, a similar one was also sent across to Ferdia, on the other side of the ford. For, if he were to defeat Ferdia, he did not want it said that his opponent died for want of proper healing. In the same way, Ferdia sent across a half-share of all the fine foods and wine that the men of Ireland provided for him. For, if he were to slay Cú Chulainn, he did not want it said that the Hound of Culann was weak from lack of food.

Next day, their battle continued. 'What weapons shall we use, today?' asked Cú Chulainn. 'You must choose,' replied Ferdia, 'for I had the choice yesterday.'

'Then let us use our heavy stabbing-spears,' said Cú Chulainn, 'for that way we may bring our conflict to a close more quickly.' So it was agreed, and from dawn until dusk they probed and pierced each other with the vicious implements. If it were the custom for birds in flight to pass through the bodies of men, they could have flown with ease through the gaping wounds left by the sharpened spear-points.

At nightfall, when the two men drew apart, they were completely exhausted. On the third morning, Cú Chulainn noticed the pain and weariness in his old companion. 'There is a dullness in your eyes and a dark shadow cast about your head and shoulders,' he said, making one last attempt to persuade his foe to leave the ford. But Ferdia was determined to continue with the fight and, as that day it was to be his choice of weapons, he suggested that they turn to their huge, death-dealing swords.

Battle commenced and, as the sun ran its course across the sky, the two men hacked away with their blades. Broad were the lumps of flesh that they cut from each other's flanks, and crimson the blood that flowed and clotted on their wounds. When night arrived they parted, sorrowful and silent, each knowing that the end was near. Their horses did not rest in the same enclosure that night, nor did the charioteers sit by the same fire.

When morning came, Ferdia rose early, donned his finest battle gear and went to wait for Cú Chulainn. 'What arms shall we try, today?' cried the latter, as he joined him.

'The choice is yours, as you know,' replied Ferdia.

'Very well, then, let us try fighting in the river,' said Cú Chulainn.

'Let us, indeed,' said Ferdia. But, though he made light of it, his heart was heavy; for he knew that Cú Chulainn had defeated all who came against him in the waters of the ford. Nonetheless, the two men began to lay into each other viciously and, until midday, they matched each other blow for blow. Then, as the pace grew hotter, Cú Chulainn leaped onto the boss of Ferdia's shield and aimed a blow at his head. But the latter cast him off, tossing him onto the bank as if he weighed no more than a babe in arms.

Immediately, Cú Chulainn leaped up again, attempting the same manoeuvre. Once more, his adversary cast him away with ease. The Hound of Culann tried the ploy a further time and, when it failed, his anger came upon him. His frame swelled up grotesquely, his features dissolved into a wicked snarl, a blinding light shone from his forehead, and a cascade of boiling blood spurted from his skull. While he was gripped in this fury, he threw himself on Ferdia and grappled with him at close quarters. Together, they thrashed about, displacing so much water from the river, that there was room enough for a king and queen to lie side by side on the bed, without getting wet.

In the midst of all this, Ferdia caught Cú Chulainn off guard with a lunge of his sword, burying it deep in the Ulsterman's side. Cú Chulainn groaned heavily, as his blood reddened the waters around him, and he called at last to Laeg to pass him the Gae Bolga, his most fearsome weapon. When Ferdia heard the mention of this dreaded name, he moved his shield instantly, protecting the lower part of his body. But it was too late. Cú Chulainn had already sent the fatal spear skimming over the water's surface. It pierced Ferdia's armour and passed right through his torso, so that its bloodied point could be seen on the other side.

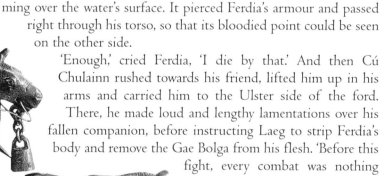

'Enough,' cried Ferdia, 'I die by that.' And then Cú Chulainn rushed towards his friend, lifted him up in his arms and carried him to the Ulster side of the ford. There, he made loud and lengthy lamentations over his fallen companion, before instructing Laeg to strip Ferdia's body and remove the Gae Bolga from his flesh. 'Before this fight, every combat was nothing more than a game to me, a piece of sport,' Cú Chulainn told his charioteer. 'Every combat was meaningless, until Ferdia came to me at the ford. This event will prey on my mind forever. For, yesterday, he was mightier than a mountain and today there is naught left of him but shadows.'

THE FINAL BATTLE

UMOURS REACHED MEDB that the Ulstermen were beginning to recover from their weakness. She urged on her forces to make their camp at Imorach Smiromrach and, once they were established there, Mac Roth was sent to scout around the area. Meanwhile, Cú Chulainn tended the wounds he had received from Ferdia.

A short time later, Mac Roth returned bearing news: 'I saw a single chariot to the north of Slieve Fuad,' he reported. 'In it, there was a naked man with silver hair, and the only weapon he carried was a heavy iron spit. But, even though he was alone, the man was goading his horses with great impatience, as if he feared that our army might move on before he had a chance to fight with us.'

'Who do you think that person might be, Fergus?' asked Ailill.

'It sounds like Cethern, son of Fintan; a hot-headed man, who knows how to wield a bloody sword,' replied Fergus. These words were truly prophetic for, moments later, Cethern's chariot thundered into the Connacht camp. With lusty blows, he set about the men of Ireland, killing more than twenty of them and receiving many wounds in exchange. As he made his escape, he had to grip his bowels, to prevent them spilling out into the chariot.

Soon, Cethern reached Cú Chulainn, who bade his friend to lie down and called for the healers. The first of these immediately announced that the wounds were so bad that they could not be cured. On hearing this, Cethern fetched the man such a blow that his jaw flew through the back of his skull. A second healer suffered the same fate, and a third until, at length, fifteen different healers had perished at the hands of the dying man.

Now Cú Chulainn sent out his charioteer to Slieve Fuad, to fetch Fingan, who was Conchobar's personal physician. Fingan was a druid, and the greatest physician in Ireland. It was said of him, that he could tell the nature of a person's ailment by the kind of smoke that came out of the house he was in. Similarly, it was said that by looking at a wound, he could name the type of person who had inflicted it.

Fingan came as requested and observed Cethern's wounds from a safe distance. 'That,' he said, pointing at one of them, 'is the work of two brothers.'

'You are right,' said Cethern, 'for it was put on me by two young men, alike as peas. They had the same yellow hair, the same green cloaks, and the same silver spears. And what of this wound?'

'A father and son made that one,' pronounced Fingan.

Cethern nodded. 'Two large men came at me. There was fire gleaming in their eyes, they carried golden swords, and they were dressed like kings.'

'That must have been Ailill and his son, Maine Andoe,' remarked Cú Chulainn.

'And this one?' enquired Cethern, pointing at the deepest and bloodiest of his wounds.

'That one was made by a proud woman,' pronounced the Druid.

'Again, you are right,' answered Cethern. 'She was a pale creature, with flowing yellow hair. She wore a crimson cloak, with a brooch of gold at her breast and two golden birds on her shoulders. In her hand, she brandished a spear that was as red as the heart of a boar.'

'Then I fear for you,' exclaimed Cú Chulainn, 'for it was Medb herself, who gave you that wound.'

Cethern turned to Fingan once more. 'So tell me, healer, what do you think of my condition?'

'I think,' said the Druid, 'that you can hardly expect to see your cows go into their next calving time or, if you do, it will not be as a fighting man.'

'Wretch!' shouted Cethern, 'your advice is no better than all the rest, and it will receive the same treatment.' With that, he lashed out strongly with his foot, sending the healer clattering down against the shaft of a chariot.

However, generous as ever, Fingan forgave Cethern for this rough handling and offered him a choice: either to spend a long time in his bed, in which case he should make a partial recovery, or else to rest for three days, which would give him strength enough for one last attack on his foes.

The decision was easy. 'I will choose the latter,' said Cethern, 'for I have no desire to leave enemies behind me and I will enjoy gaining my revenge.' So the Druid then prepared a healing bath, using a broth made from animal bones, and at the end of three days Cethern was well enough to launch his final assault on his enemies.

But the men of Ireland had heard of his coming, and they quickly devised a plan. They took Ailill's cloak and crown and placed these on a pillar-stone near their camp. So that when Cethern made his attack, in the half-light of early morning, he mistook the pillar for Ailill and plunged the sword right through it. Then, as he realized his mistake, Medb's people closed in and made an end of him.

While these events were occurring, Cú Chulainn's father, Sualtam, came to see how he was faring against the men of Connacht. He was much saddened when he saw how the battle with Ferdia had left him. There was scarcely a part of his son's body that had not some wound or gash upon it. And, although the healers had placed grasses and charms on these sores, it was clear that the lad was still in great pain. He could not bear to feel the touch of clothing against his skin and, so, had put hazel twigs about his body, to keep the roughness of the robe from his flesh.

When Sualtam saw these things, he began to grieve for his son. But Cú Chulainn would have none of this and urged him to travel instead to Emain Macha. 'Go to the Ulstermen, and tell them to enter into battle with Medb's armies at once, for I can no longer defend them.'

Sualtam readily obeyed, making haste to reach Conchobar's capital. There, he bellowed out his warning: 'We are under threat, men of Ulster. Men are being murdered, women carried off, and cattle seized.' He proclaimed these words from the slope of the enclosure at Emain Macha, but there was no response. So, he moved inside the fort and repeated the warning a second time. But again, no reply was forthcoming. Then Sualtam came to the Mound of the Hostages, the very heart of Emain Macha, and delivered his message for the third and final time. But, as before, silence was the only response.

There was a reason for this strange behaviour. For, amongst the Ulstermen, there was a custom that none should speak except to Conchobar, and that Conchobar himself would not speak before the three druids. One of these now addressed Sualtam: 'Who is responsible for the atrocities you describe?'

'Ailill, son of Máta, is the man. He has enslaved your people as far as Dun Sobairce; he has stolen your cows and carried off your women. Cú Chulainn alone has held them back from the plain of Muirthemne, these past three months. But now his wounds lie heavy upon him and he can defend your lands no longer,' answered Sualtam.

'Death should be the reward of any man, who speaks in such an insolent manner to the king,' said one of the druids.

'It should,' agreed Conchobar, 'although there is some truth in what Sualtam says. Ailill's people have been harassing us for three months.' The tameness of this answer incensed Sualtam and he hurried away. In his haste, however, he tripped over his own shield and its razor-sharp edge sliced his head from his shoulders. Servants picked it up, placed it on the shield, and carried it back into Conchobar's presence. There, the severed head spoke and repeated its warning.

Now the king regretted his former actions and made a vow before the men of Ulster. 'Unless the sky with all its stars falls down around our heads, unless the ground breaks open at our feet, unless the broad seas flood the earth, I swear before you all that I will return every cow to its shed and every woman to her dwelling-place.'

CELTIC CROSSES

Detail of the Cross of the Scriptures, County Offaly, Ireland.

STANDING STONES had long been the focus of solar cults throughout western Europe, before pre-Christian Celts starting erecting monumental pillar-statues, placing them in sanctuaries and burial places. Their general shape suggests that they were meant to represent trees, which were held in great reverence by the early Celts. They survived the coming of the Christian era, as missionaries did not wish to upset potential converts by destroying their shrines. Instead, they Christianized the stones by carving crosses on them, a custom said to have been introduced by St Patrick himself. In the sixth century, craftsmen began sculpting them into the form of free-standing crosses.

Spirals, interlacing and key patterns were all borrowed from Celtic metalwork and, in some cases, the affinity with secular artefacts was even closer. The prominent bosses on the cross at Ahenny, for instance, have been likened to rivets. By the tenth century, however, the depiction of figures was becoming more common and this trend was to culminate in the great Crosses of the Scriptures, shown above.

TARA

The Mound of the Hostages, a passage-tomb on the sacred site of Tara.

TARA IS A prehistoric burial site in County Meath, famed as the legendary capital of the high kings of Ireland, and a holy site for thousands of years. Here, according to tradition, elaborate rites were carried out between the future high king of Tara and the goddess of sovereignty. Medb, for example, was said to have participated in a ritual union with nine of the high kings, preventing the rule of any candidates who refused to mate with her. Another test was provided by the Stone of Fál, which screamed when it was touched by the rightful heir. There are claims that Cormac mac Art, a leading figure in the Fionn Cycle (see page 76), established a sumptuous court at Tara and a lavish festival was also regularly celebrated at Samhain, on 1 November.

In the fifth century, the place was occupied by Niall of the Nine Hostages and it was here that his pagan son, King Laoghaire, was supposed to have been confronted by St Patrick. After this, Tara's importance appears to have declined. Nonetheless, the twelfth-century *Book of Leinster* contains an illustration of the Banqueting Hall at Tara, which begs comparison with Arthur's Round Table, and the site has always been seen as a symbol of national unity.

Excavations have revealed traces of wooden buildings, dating from between the first and third centuries AD, and there is a standing stone which may be associated with the Stone of Fál. Some sources argue that the latter was Jacob's pillow, transported to Ireland by Israelite refugees; others say that the real stone was carried to Scotland by a king of Ulster. According to this theory, the monolith became known as the Stone of Scone, the coronation stone which has long been held in Westminster Abbey.

Now that his resolution had been made, Conchobar wasted no further time in mustering the men of Ulster. That very day, he and Celtchair set out from Emain with thrice fifty of their chariots, bidding others to come and join them.

As the armies moved forward to meet each other, Cú Chulainn was lying on his bed, still stricken with his extensive wounds. From the sounds on the plain, however, he could tell that the army of the Ulstermen was drawing near and that battle would soon commence. He could also hear the croaking voice of the Morrigán, as she taunted the warriors of both sides, boasting that she would soon be picking the dead flesh from off their bones. Cú Chulainn was stirred by all these things happening, and he wanted to rise up and join the fray. However, his underlings feared that his wounds would open up again, so they tied ropes and fastenings about him, to make sure that he could not move.

Then Cú Chulainn called out to his charioteer, to watch the progress of the battle and report to him all that occurred. So Laeg described how a small herd of cattle had broken away from Ailill's camp, and how the servants of both sides had rushed to try and take control of it.

'That small herd on the plain is the harbinger of a great battle,' answered Cú Chulainn, 'for that will certainly be the Brown Bull of Cooley with all his heifers, who is the cause of all this strife and anguish.'

Then, as the sun rose higher in the sky, Laeg went out again, to see how the battle was faring. For, now, the two armies had clashed in earnest and were engaged in bitter hand-to-hand combat. Throughout the morning hours, neither side gained any advantage. So, while Medb's warriors made a breach in one part of the Ulster defences, this was soon matched by a surge from Conchobar's men in another part of the line. Cú Chulainn lamented greatly when he heard this, swearing that his presence would have made all the difference.

Now when Medb saw that the battle was reaching stalemate, she turned to Fergus. 'It is time,' she said, 'that you went out to challenge Conchobar, to repay us for all the hospitality you have had in Connacht.' On these words Fergus took up his sword and cut a swathe through the ranks of Ulster, killing a hundred men in his first attack. Medb and Ailill followed in his wake and, between them, they forced the Ulstermen to retreat three times.

Conchobar was alarmed at this turn of events, and he went to see what was driving his people back. Soon, he found himself right in front of Fergus. Swiftly, he raised up his shield, Ochain the Screamer. Lavish to behold, with its four gold horns and its four gold coverings, the Ochain was an enchanted shield that cried out when its master was in danger. Three times Fergus brought his blade down with full force on Conchobar, but the Ochain shield was not even dented. Instead, it screamed aloud, and all the shields of Ulster screamed with it.

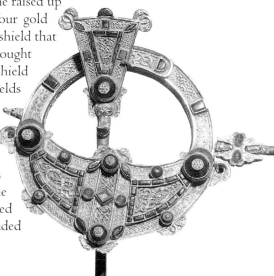

'Who holds this shield?' asked Fergus.

'A better man than you,' was Conchobar's reply. 'I am the one who drove you into exile.'

Then Fergus knew that it was Conchobar before him and his fury was raised to a greater pitch. He again lifted his sword, the mighty Cladcholg, and was about to strike, when Cormac rushed forward and threw himself at Fergus's feet. On his knees, he pleaded

HEAD-HUNTING

Horse harness decorated with many heads. Celtic warriors collected severed heads, attaching them to the saddles of their horses.

MUCH ATTENTION has been devoted to the Celts' interest in head-hunting, partly no doubt due to ghoulish curiosity, but also because it gives firm evidence that some of their activities transcended national boundaries. Several classical authors remarked on the subject with ill-concealed fascination. Strabo, for example, reported: 'There is that custom, barbarous and exotic ... that when they depart from battle they carry off the heads of their enemies ... and nail the spectacle to the entrance of their houses.' This corresponds closely to some passages in the *Tain*, where Cú Chulainn decapitates his foes and proudly displays their severed heads on the side of his chariot. It also accords well with findings at Entremont and Roquepertuse, two shrines situated in southern Gaul. These featured porticoes decorated with carvings of severed heads and niches containing genuine skulls. For the Celts, the head was important because it housed the soul and could have talismanic properties. Irish, Welsh and Breton tales all gave accounts of 'living' severed heads, that could speak, eat and drink; the tale of Bran the Blessed in the *Mabinogion* is probably the most colourful of these.

with the Ulsterman not to betray his native land by striking down its king. Fergus paused for a moment and then agreed, provided that Conchobar retreated from the head of his forces. Then instead of severing the king's head, he turned his sword aside and sliced the tops off three small hills instead.

Cú Chulainn, meanwhile, had heard the sound of Ochain's screams and called out to his charioteer: 'Who has dared to strike three blows against the king?'

'It is Fergus, that most valiant of warriors, and now his sword is laying low the men of Ulster,' replied Laeg.

On hearing this, Cú Chulainn mustered all that was left of his remaining strength. He threw off the ropes that were binding him and scattered the healing grasses in the air. Then he called for his weapons to be fetched and his twenty-seven tunics to be placed about him. As these were being tied, the fury came upon him, opening up all his old wounds. But, in his frenzied state, Cú Chulainn felt no pain or weakness. Indeed, such was his impatience, that he did not wait for his chariot to be harnessed. Instead, he lifted the carriage onto his back and went towards the battle.

Once in the fray, he used the chariot he carried as a massive club, smiting all who came before him. Before long, he came face to face with Fergus. Now, his anger cooled and he spoke with the mild words of a foster-son: 'Go back, Fergus. Remember your promise to me.'

'Who is it that calls to me thus, in the heat of battle?' asked Fergus.

'It is I, Cú Chulainn,' the boy replied. 'Remember how you came to me at the ford, Fergus. You had no sword in your scabbard and yet you asked me to yield to you. In return, you promised to yield to me on another occasion. That time has come. Yield to me now, Fergus. Remember your promise.'

'I remember it,' he said. With these words, Fergus turned away and left the field, taking with him his troop of three thousand men. And all the men of Ireland turned, when they saw this, and took to their heels. Cú Chulainn and the Ulstermen pursued them, slaughtering them as they fled. It had been midday when the Hound of Culann arrived on the scene, and the sun was just beginning to set when the last of his foes made their escape over the ford.

Fergus watched this from a distance, as Medb's army was scattered to the winds. 'All this comes from following the lead of a woman,' he muttered to himself. 'A mare will always lead a herd astray.'

On the day after the battle, the survivors came to witness the meeting of the two great bulls. For Medb had been determined that, whoever won the war, the Brown Bull would go back with her to Cruachan. So, the great prize was taken into Connacht, to a place that was later named Tarbga or 'Bull-sorrow', after the combat that had taken place there. Once the two bulls caught sight of each other, all their old rivalries came back to haunt them. They remembered only too well their battles: first as swineherds, then as ravens, as water creatures, as warriors, as phantoms and, lastly, as eels. Now, in their final guises, they charged at each other instantly. So violent was this rush, that poison-tongued Bricriu was trampled to death.

Within moments, the beasts had locked horns, each seeking to gain an early advantage. This went to the Brown Bull of Cooley as it planted its powerful hoof on the head of the White-horned Bull and refused to budge. The animals remained in this position for a day and a night, until Fergus took a stick to the Brown Bull, forcing it to release its foe.

The battle of the Bulls continued deep into the night, so that the men of Connacht could no longer stay awake to watch the contest. But, the snorting, the bellowing and the constant clashing of the bulls' heads still echoed loudly in the darkness, and no one in the province had much sleep that night. When morning came, it was clear that the Brown Bull of Cooley was the victor. All that could be found of the White-horned Bull were the bloodied remains of its loins, its liver and its shoulder-blade, which were lodged in the horns of the Brown Bull.

Then, there arose a general cry from the people that the Bull of Cooley – this creature that had been the cause of so much slaughter – should itself be slain. Fergus would not allow this, however, and said that the Bull should be left to go in peace. No one dared to dispute this and, so, the beast headed back towards its native land. When it came to the ford of Ath Luain, it stopped for a drink and the two loins of the White-horned Bull fell into the water. The shoulder-blade fell

off in the same way at Findlethe and the liver was dropped at Tromma. Eventually, the Brown Bull reached the top of Slieve Breagh and, from there, it gazed across towards the hills of Cooley. The sight of its native land caused a great stirring in the Bull. The blood rushed through its veins and, with a final bellow, its heart burst and it died.

After the cattle raid of Cooley, Medb and Ailill made their peace with Conchobar. The Ulstermen went back to Emain Macha in great triumph and, for the next seven years, there was friendship between Connacht and Ulster. No wounding of men or stealing of cattle marred this peaceful understanding. But Medb had not forgiven the Hound of Culann for thwarting her ambitions. So, during the years of peace, she sought out others who had a grievance against him: widows who had lost their husbands at the ford; sons and daughters who had lost their father during one of his onslaughts. First, she sought out the three one-eyed daughters of Calatin, for their loss had been the greatest. Cú Chulainn had slain their father and their twenty-seven brothers in a single afternoon. And Medb spurred them on to take revenge. 'Make a journey through the whole world,' she urged them, 'to get knowledge of spells and enchantments from those that have it. Then, when the opportunity arises, you can avenge your father.' The sisters obeyed, travelling to Alban and to every other country. At the end of the year, they returned to Medb and told her of the wonders they had learned; how, with secret words, they could make terrifying visions of war.

Then Medb sought out Lugaid, the son of Curoi, and Erc, the son of Cairbre. Both had lost their fathers to the sword of Cú Chulainn and both were eager to seek revenge. So Medb told them to gather armies and bring them to Cruachan. There, they feasted and made merry for three days and three nights before setting out on their mission. This time, however, Medb left Fergus behind, fearing that he would assist Cú Chulainn in some way.

Soon, Conchobar got word that there were skirmishes on the borders of his province. There was little he could do since, once again, the Ulstermen were in their weakness, but he sent out messengers to alert Cú Chulainn. They found him at Baile's Strand, where he was trying to bring down sea-birds with his sling. The birds all flew past him and escaped, however, and this made Cú Chulainn unhappy, for he knew there must be some bad meaning in this event.

Now Conchobar had heard of Medb's plan to use enchantments on his young champion, so he placed him in the care of Niamh, instructing her to hide him in her house at Glean-na-Bodhar. Thus, when the daughters of Calatin arrived at Emain Macha, they could not find him lodging with Conchobar or with any of his men. However, the deformed sisters had acquired many strange powers. Using one of these, they transformed themselves into a moaning wind that gusted through the province, searching through every wood and valley, every cave and secret path, until at length they found Cú Chulainn at Glean-na-Bodhar.

Once there, the wicked sisters sat cross-legged on the lawn and began making their charms. They tugged at the grass and cast it into the air, chanting as they did so. In this way, they gave each thistle-stalk, each slender reed and each withered leaf the appearance of an armed warrior. And they put into the air the sounds of battle, trumpet calls and clashing swords and the screams of dying men. When Cú Chulainn heard these, he was convinced that Ulster was under threat and he went to find his sword, to join the fight. But Niamh and her maidens held him back, warning him that these were just enchantments to confuse him, and made him promise not to leave the house. Then, they played sweet music for him, to drown out the sounds of battle.

For three days, Cú Chulainn remained in this confusion, constantly hearing the noise of battle in his head. Then one of the daughters of Calatin put on the shape of Niamh and went to see Cú Chulainn in his chamber. 'Rise up,' she said, 'for Muirthemne is burning, and Emer and your household are under serious threat. And all of Ulster will lay the blame on me, saying that I hindered you. Go now and help them.' So, released from his promise, Cú Chulainn left Niamh's house and started on the fatal journey to Muirthemne.

As Cú Chulainn rushed homeward, many bad omens impeded his progress. His favourite brooch fell from his cloak and stabbed him in the foot. Then, when he stopped to see his mother, Dechtire, and was offered wine, the goblets contained nothing but blood. At last, as he approached the armies of Lugaid and Erc, he came upon the daughters of Calatin. They were now in the shape of three old hags, roasting a dog on a spit.

'Stay a while, Cú Chulainn, and take meat with us,' one of them cried out.

'I thank you,' he replied, 'but I cannot. I have urgent business.'

'If we had a great cooking-hearth or a large feasting table, you would not treat us so. It is only because we have little to offer you that you will not stop. But, he that shows no respect for lowly folk will get no respect himself, however great a man he may be.'

So Cú Chulainn descended from his chariot and sat with them for a while. One of the hags gave him a shoulder-bone, and he took it with his left hand and rested it on his left thigh. Then he ate from it and, as the morsels passed his lips, the strength ebbed from the left side of his body.

Cú Chulainn rose up instantly, knowing he had been enchanted. Soon after he left the hags, he fell into the ambush set by Lugaid and Erc. He gave a good account of himself, bloodying many a head with his sword, but the weakness put on him by the three sisters proved too much. A spear from Lugaid went through him, and he knew he had received a deadly wound. He staggered to a pillar-stone and tied himself to it, so he could meet his death standing up rather than lying down.

Still, his enemies were afraid to come near to him, fearing that he would strike them a final blow. Then, at last, the Morrigán came as a bird and settled on his shoulder, to show them that he was dead. Warily, Lugaid approached, in order to behead Cú Chulainn. But, as he raised his arm, the sword slipped from the hand of the Hound of Culann, severing Lugaid's right hand.

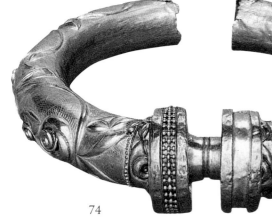

Cú Chulainn's death was avenged by Conall Cearnach, and his head was taken to Emer. She cleansed it of all wounds and then wrapped it in a silken cloth, to be buried with an Ogham marker set upon the grave. And the thrice fifty queens that loved Cú Chulainn saw him in a vision, riding in his chariot and singing the music of the sidhe.

THE FIONN CYCLE

THE FIONN OR FENIAN cycle of stories presents an eclectic mix of heroic battles and enchanting love stories, all relating to Ireland's legendary Celtic militia, the *fianna*. The tales are traditionally set in the third century AD and their central hero is Fionn mac Cumhaill (frequently anglicised as Finn mac Cool). He leads his elite band of warriors around Ireland, where they encounter a magical array of giants, serpents and other monsters. While the *Táin* was set principally in Ulster, the action of the Fionn Cycle is located mainly in Leinster and Munster. The stories are more romantic in character, too, reinforcing the argument that they helped inspire many of the medieval Arthurian legends. The cycle also includes a number of tales about Oisin and, for this reason, the collection is sometimes known as the Ossianic Cycle.

THE PLOT

The Fionn Cycle is set against a background of two feuding clans, the Clan Baoisgne and the Clan Morna, both struggling to be recognized as the true Fenians. Cumhaill, the leader of the former tribe, is defeated and killed, but his wife gives birth in secret to a son. The boy is named Demna, but he becomes better known as Finn, meaning 'fair youth'. The boy is raised in a forest, to protect him from the vengeance of the Clan Morna. But, as he grows older, the youth is determined to seek out his father's killer and gain his inheritance. The story of Finn and the Salmon begins at this stage, as the lad goes to Finnegas, to seek his help. The events related in 'Diarmaid and Gráinne' occur much later in his career, when he has performed many feats of daring with the Fianna. He is now an ageing widower.

THE CHARACTERS

Finn mac Cumhaill (Finn mac Cool) The leader of the elite war band the *fianna*, and hero of the Fionn cycle.

Gráinne The wilful daughter of Cormac mac Art, the High King at Tara, in dangerous pursuit of Diarmaid

Diarmaid O'Duibhne Finn's cousin, a Fenian Adonis. Loved by Gráinne, he is placed under a druid's spell.

Oisin Second son of Finn, acknowledged as the greatest warrior in Ireland, and one of the bravest champions of the *fianna*.

Oenghus A Celtic love god, the helper of lovers and himself in love.

The Dagda The father of all the gods. His title means 'the good god'.

Boann A water goddess and mother of the love god, Oenghus. Ireland's River Boyne is named after her.

Finnegas and Daire Learned druids and advisors to Finn mac Cumhaill.

Cormac mac Art The High King at Tara, said to have ruled from 254-277.

DIARMAID AND GRAINNE

ESPITE FINN'S SUCCESS as a warrior, a feeling of great lone-
liness came upon him after his wife died. His people, therefore, searched for a suitor. They chose Gráinne, daughter of
Cormac mac Art, the high king of Tara, to be his bride.

Once the betrothal was agreed Finn travelled to Tara to
claim his new wife. He brought with him a fine company,
including all the great warriors of the fianna. Gráinne cast
an eye along their ranks, as they were seated together at the
banquet. Then she leaned across the table and spoke to
Daire, one of Finn's druids. 'Tell me,' she asked, 'why is it,
do you think, that Finn seeks my hand for himself, rather
than for someone like Oisin, who is much closer to my age?'

Daire was greatly embarrassed by this question and made
no answer. But Gráinne persisted, asking the unfortunate druid to name the young men present at
the feast. Reluctantly, the aged seer obeyed, describing the qualities of all those indicated. And
Diarmaid, Dubne's grandson, was among the ones described.

Then Gráinne motioned to her serving-woman and sent her to fetch a golden drinking-horn
from her chamber. When it was brought, she had it filled with wine and offered it to Finn. He
drank deeply from it, and then passed it to Cormac. But Gráinne had placed a sleeping draught
in the vessel and, shortly afterwards, all those who had partaken of it were slumped over the table.

Now Gráinne seized her opportunity. She rose from her place at the table and went to sit
between Oisin and Diarmaid. At first, she addressed the former, asking him if he would be willing to court her. Oisin was shocked at the suggestion and answered her hotly: 'No, I would not;
for you are betrothed to Finn.'

Then Gráinne said to Diarmaid. 'And you, my lord. Would you accept my love, as Oisin refuses it?'

'No,' he replied. 'I would never meddle with any woman who was promised to my master.'

'In that case,' she continued, 'I place you under a geis, a druid's spell. Take me away with you this
night, or you will suffer the consequences.'

Diarmaid was astonished at this turn of events. 'Why me?' he asked. 'Why, of all the men in
Ireland, do you choose to place me in such danger?'

SAMHAIN

Panel from the Gundestrop Cauldron: the dancers on the god's shoulders are surrounded by leaping flames.

SAMHAIN WAS AN important fire festival which was celebrated on the evening of 31 October and throughout the following day. Old fires were extinguished and had to be ceremonially relit from a sacred flame, tended by druids. Samhain also marked the beginning of the new year, but it seems to have been linked with the pastoral cycle rather than the solar or agricultural year. Therefore, the new year coincided with the period when herds were brought in from the fields and selected for breeding or slaughter. Samhain was also a festival of the dead. At the turning of the year, the souls of the departed returned to the world of the living and warmed themselves in their former homes. Less benevolent spirits were also released from the Otherworld and had to be either appeased or expelled.

Samhain was later Christianized as the feast of All Saints' Day, but traces of the older, pagan traditions have survived in the popular celebrations at Hallowe'en.

'Because of the day that I first saw you. There was a hurling match between the fianna and the men of Tara. You were in the crowd, looking on with the other men. But, as the game began to go against your compatriots, you grabbed a hurling-stick from one of them and joined the game. You scored three goals that day, outstripping all your fellows in strength and skill. I watched you from my window and, ever since that moment, I have loved you.'

'I am flattered,' said Diarmaid, 'but I still don't see why you cannot be satisfied with Finn, who has performed so many noble deeds in the past. Anyway, there is little choice in the matter, for the keys of Tara are in his keeping this night. So, there is no way that we can leave without them.'

'That is a poor excuse,' said Gráinne. 'We can leave by a wicket-gate leading from my apartments.'

'Not so,' countered Diarmaid, 'for it is one of my gesa that I may not leave a royal mansion through a wicket-gate.'

'Then you may leap over it,' she said, 'for I am sure that a warrior as fine as you must be skilled in the art of vaulting.' And with these words, she went off to her chamber to get ready to depart.

Diarmaid, meanwhile, turned to his companions for advice. 'What must I do?' he asked Oisin, 'for I have no wish to betray your father.'

'You have no choice in the matter,' Oisin replied. 'You must observe the geis. But flee now. For, when Finn discovers what has happened, he will surely look for vengeance.'

Diarmaid obeyed these words and, while Finn and Cormac slept, he and Gráinne escaped.

But little did the lovers know how long and difficult their flight would be. Finn pursued them relentlessly and, for years on end, they lived in constant danger. And the greatest of these perils occurred when they entered the forest of Dooros and found the fairy quicken tree.

Now Diarmaid thought it would be a wise idea if they hid in the forest of Dooros. For, it was well known that a magic quicken tree grew in this place. This had sprouted up from a berry which the Tuatha De Danaan had dropped by accident, and anyone who ate the fruit of this tree was instantly rejuvenated and cured of all disease. To prevent this, the Tuatha De Danaan placed a guard on the tree, a fearsome giant called Sharvan the Surly. This monster had a single, fiery eye in the centre of his smoke-black forehead. He was skilled in magic and impervious to water, fire and to attack from ordinary weapons. The only way he could be killed was with three blows from his own club, which was chained to an iron girdle on his body. Nor did Sharvan ever stray far from the quicken tree. By day, he sat in its shade and, by night, he slept high up among the branches.

Such was the terror that Sharvan inspired in everyone, that no one dared to enter the forest. Even the warriors of the fianna did not hunt there. It seemed to Diarmaid, therefore, that it was a perfect place to hide from Finn. So, he made a pact with the giant. He and Gráinne would be allowed to shelter in the forest, provided that they did not touch the berries on the magic tree.

But Finn came to hear of this ruse, and he hatched a plot to foil it. Two noble warriors, Aed and Angus, had recently approached him, seeking to join the ranks of the fianna. So, Finn proposed a test. They were either to bring him the head of Diarmaid or else some berries from the quicken tree. Gloomily, the warriors decided that Diarmaid would offer them the easier option, and so they went to the forest of Dooros to seek him out. There, they challenged Diarmaid to a wrestling match, but it proved an uneven contest and the two men were soon bound and gagged.

Diarmaid, for his own part, had a different problem. Gráinne was now with child and she had developed a terrible craving for the fruit of the quicken tree. Indeed, it was so fierce, that Diarmaid feared she might die of it. So, despite the danger, he went to try and pluck some berries from the tree. On learning this, Aed and Angus offered to come and help him and, even though he thought they would be of little use, Diarmaid loosened their bonds and told them to follow him.

Sharvan was sleeping when they arrived at the tree. So Diarmaid woke him up and explained the situation, begging him for just a few of the berries to help Gráinne. But the giant was unmoved. 'I care not whether she lives or dies,' was his response. 'No mortal may taste the fruit of this tree.' With that, Diarmaid hurled himself at the beast, catching him by surprise. Then, taking up Sharvan's club, he dealt him three stout blows, the last of which dashed out his brains. After this, Diarmaid ordered Aed and Angus to bury the body, and he allowed them to take away a few of the berries to show to Finn, as proof that they had passed his test. He, meanwhile, climbed up the quicken tree with Gráinne and they stayed in Sharvan's dwelling-place, high up among the branches. There, they ate the berries, which tasted infinitely sweeter than those on the lower branches.

But Finn was suspicious when he saw the fruit. When he placed it near to his nose, he was sure that he could detect the smell of his bitter foe. From this, he deduced that Sharvan must be dead and that it was safe to travel into the forest of Dooros. So, gathering the men of the fianna about him, he set off to find the fairy quicken tree.

They arrived at the tree in the heat of the day, and Finn ordered his men to dismount and rest in the shade, until dusk. He settled down to a game of chess with Oisin, underneath the branches of the quicken tree. They played for an hour, until the game reached a critical stage. Then Finn teased Oisin, saying: 'If you make the right move now, you can win the game. Can you see it, my son?' But Oisin just stared at the board, puzzled by what to do next. Diarmaid, however, who had been watching the game from above, spotted the right move. And, taking careful aim, he dropped a berry on the crucial piece. Oisin took this hint, played the correct move and won the game. Two further games were then played, each one following a similar pattern. After his third defeat, Finn stood up. 'I am not surprised that you have done so well as you had Diarmaid's assistance.'

Oisin scoffed heartily at this declaration, and he said: 'Your jealousy must have made you completely blind. Do you really think that he would linger in this place, knowing that you were here?'

'Yes, I do. And Diarmaid

can confirm it for us.' With this, he looked up to where the lovers were hiding.

'As always, Finn, your judgment is sound,' replied Diarmaid, brushing the leaves aside, so that his enemy could see himself and Gráinne. Then, he boldly kissed Gráinne three times.

'You shall pay for those kisses with your head,' cried Finn, and he offered magnificent rewards to any man who would climb the tree and send Diarmaid hurtling down.

'Let me be the chosen man,' called out Garva of Slieve Cua, as he scrambled up the trunk and disappeared amid the leaves.

Now, at this point, Oenghus arrived in a breeze to rescue the lovers. As Diarmaid kicked the foolhardy Garva out of the tree, Oenghus changed Garva's face and form, so that he resembled Diarmaid, Finn's quarry. The men of the fianna rejoiced, as they tore his head from his body and carried it away in triumph. Before they realized their mistake, Oenghus spirited the lovers away to his palace.

SWANS

S WANS FIGURE extensively in Celtic lore, often carrying magical overtones. Their Otherworldly status is usually emphasized by chains of gold or silver around their necks. Many of the early stories also feature humans transformed into swans. In the 'Dream of Oenghus', the maiden Caer lives in the shape of a swan and can only be wooed if her lover adopts the same guise. Another famous tale concerns the tragic fate of the children of Lir. The latter was an Irish sea god whose children were transformed into swans by their wicked stepmother, using a druid's wand. The fact that their enchantment was ended by the sound of a Christian bell indicates that the surviving version of the Lir tale is comparatively late. Nevertheless, swans were important throughout the Celtic era and images of them have been found on ritual vessels, which date back as far as the Hallstatt period, c. 700–500 BC.

OENGHUS IN LOVE

ENGHUS, THE SON OF the Dagda, was asleep in his bed one night, when a beautiful young girl appeared to him in a dream. She seemed so real that he stretched out his arm to touch her and, as he did so, the vision melted away. The maiden's face remained clear in his mind, however, and throughout the next day he could not banish her beautiful image from his thoughts.

On the following night, the maiden returned to his dreams. This time, she brought a tiny harp with her, and she sang him the sweetest songs he had ever heard. Oenghus rested well that night but, as dawn began to break, the girl vanished again and his heart was heavy. No food passed his lips that day and his spirit was troubled with thoughts of her.

This train of events continued, night after night, for a whole year. Throughout this time, Oenghus pined for the lovely maid and his people became concerned for him. Physicians were summoned, but they could not put a name to his sickness or discover any cure for it. Eventually, Fergne, the most famous of the healers, was brought to see him. Straightaway, he recognized that the ailment lay in Oenghus's mind, not his body. Taking him to one side, he told him of his finding: 'I think it is for the love of some woman that you are wasting away like this.'

'That is true,' replied Oenghus. 'I see that my sickness has betrayed me.' Whereupon, he confessed all to Fergne, telling him of the beautiful maid who came to him each night to haunt his dreams and his every waking thought.

The physician explained these things to Boann, the mother of Oenghus, and she sent her people to search through all of Ireland for the girl. For a whole year, they hunted in every corner of the land; on remote mountain-tops, in the darkest depths of the forest, and in the meanest of dwelling-places. At the end of all that time, they had still found no sign of her. Meanwhile, Oenghus continued to waste away.

Then Fergne made another suggestion. 'Send to Bodb, in his fairy-dwelling in Munster. He is the king of all the sidhe and no knowledge can be hidden from him.' This was done, and Bodb agreed to use whatever lay within his power to find the girl. He proved as good as his word. At the end of the following year, messengers arrived to say that the maid had been discovered at Lough Beul Draguin, at the Harp of Cliach.

Oenghus sped to the place as if he had wings attached to his feet. There, at the water's edge, he spied thrice fifty maidens linked in pairs with silver chains. Alone among them all was the girl that haunted his dreams, whom he had sought for three long years. She had her own necklet, beautifully made of burnished gold.

'Do you know her name?' asked Oenghus.

'Certainly,' replied Bodb, 'she is Caer, the daughter of Ethal Anbual, from the fairy-dwelling of Uaman in Connacht. But you may not speak with her now. First, you must ask the permission of Medb and Ailill, for it is in their territory that she lives.'

So the Dagda took his son, Oenghus, and they went together to see Medb and Ailill at Cruachan. There, they were made very welcome and a great feast was laid before them while messengers were sent to fetch Ethal Anbual. But when they asked him to hand over his daughter, he shook his head and said: 'I cannot, there is a power over her and her maidens that far exceeds my authority.'

'What power is this?' Ailill demanded.

'It is an enchantment,' he replied. 'She and her maidens must reside in the shape of birds for one year, and in their own form throughout the year that follows. Go seek her next summer at Lough Beul Draguin, and you will see if I am telling the truth.' The sincerity of his words was apparent to all and he was released.

Oenghus waited with much impatience for the summer, hardly daring to believe that his long search might be drawing to a close. When the time came, he hurried to the lough and watched in wonder as thrice fifty swans coasted on the water. Each had a silver chain, save only one, and Oenghus called out anxiously to her.

'Caer. Come over and speak with me, I implore you.'

'Who is it, that summons me thus?' she asked.

'It is I, Oenghus. Please come and talk with me.'

'Only if you promise that I may return to the water, if ever I wish it.'

'I swear it,' Oenghus replied.

On hearing this assurance, the maid swam over and laid her downy head in Oenghus's lap. Then, to show her that he would keep true to his oath, he proceeded to turn himself into a swan. Together, they glided into the lough and swam round it three times. After that, they spread their wings and rose up from the water, flying all the way to the Dagda's palace at Brugh na Bóinne. And, as they flew, their voices made a honeyed sound that was so sweet to the ear, that all who heard it were gently lulled into a deep sleep which lasted for three days and three nights.

Caer stayed with Oenghus for ever afterwards. And, for the favours they had shown him, Oenghus always held a great bond of friendship with Medb and Ailill. It was because of this allegiance that he offered them assistance, during the great cattle raid of Cooley.

FINN AND THE SALMON

 AKING HIS WAY towards the River Boyne, Finn now headed for the home of Finnegas or Finn Eces, the druid. Finnegas had lived in this place for seven years, hoping to catch sight of the Salmon of Knowledge. For, it had been prophesied that whoever ate the whole salmon would be blessed with boundless wisdom. This same prophecy also stated that the salmon would be eaten by one called Finn, and Finnegas had supposed that this referred to him. He had no suspicions, therefore, when a lad called Demna asked to become his pupil.

Then, one day, the druid witnessed a sight that brought him great joy. There, by the river's edge, lay the fish he had been waiting for. It was much larger than a normal salmon and, on its shiny skin, all the colours of the rainbow seemed to dance and swirl. Taking it up, Finnegas carried the salmon back to his house and told his pupil to cook it, but forbade him to taste any of it.

Finn did as he was told and soon the smell of cooked salmon wafted through the house. Finnegas sat at the table and, as the fish was brought to him, he asked the lad if he had tasted it.

'No,' Finn replied, but he hesitated, so the druid made him tell all. 'I have not eaten any part of it,' he continued, 'but, as I was cooking the fish, I burned my thumb on it and sucked it to ease the pain.'

The druid was perplexed. 'You say your name is Demna and, yet, according to the prophecy, it must be Finn. For, now that you have tasted it, only you can eat the salmon in its entirety.'

Finn then told about his nickname and Finnegas understood it all. He bade the lad sit down and eat the salmon. Finn did as he was told. By this means, he came to have the power of divination that was within the Salmon of Knowledge. After this, whenever he wanted to know the future, he just chanted the sacred poem, the teinm laida, and placed a finger on the Tooth of Knowledge. Soon after this, Finn left the druid and continued on his travels. In time, these brought him to the royal court at Tara, where he was warmly greeted by Conn. It was not long before Finn found an opportunity to repay the generosity of his host.

One day Conn rose up from his seat to address his people. 'My friends, the day draws near when we shall be at Samhain time. On that dreaded day, the goblin Aillen

will come amongst us and lull us all to sleep with his sweet fairy music. Then, while we slumber, he will set light to our beloved Tara and reduce it to ashes. Each year he does this, and each year we rebuild our stronghold from nothing. Is there none among you who can save us from this fate?'

'I will help you,' replied Finn, for there was in the company a man named Fiacha mac Conga. He had been a friend of Finn's father and offered to lend the lad an enchanted spear that he kept. He showed him how to use its magic properties, but warned the youngster that Aillen was a dangerous foe to fight and would kill him if he failed. The days went by and Samhain time came round. The dead rose from their tombs and spirits from the Otherworld were released. As darkness fell, the goblin Aillen arrived at Tara and began to play his song of enchantment.

Immediately, Finn followed the instructions that Fiacha had given him. He stripped the spear of its coverings and placed its sharpened point against his forehead. This enabled him to stay awake, while all of Conn's guards fell into a heavy slumber. At last, when Aillen thought that all was safe, he stepped out of the shadows and opened wide his jaws. From these, there came a roaring flame, hot enough to turn the court of Tara into cinders. But swiftly, Finn leaped forward to face him. He raised his cloak to meet the flame and all of Aillen's heat was spent on it.

When the goblin saw that his magic had failed him, he turned and ran. Like a demon, he sped to his fairy-dwelling at Slieve Fuad, thinking that no one would dare to follow. But Finn pursued him and, when he came within reach, he hurled Fiacha's magic spear. His aim was true and Aillen's slithery frame was nailed to the nearest tree. Now Finn beheaded him and placed his ugly skull upon a pole. This he brought back in triumph to Tara, where Conn and all his people honoured him.

CELTIC ILLUMINATION

THE LAST GREAT flowering of Celtic art took place with manuscript illumination. This owed much of its impetus to the gradual conversion of the British Isles, which was carried out on two separate fronts. There were the official papal delegations, headed by figures such as St Augustine in England and Palladius in Ireland, competing alongside the more autonomous missions of St Columba, St Patrick and St Aidan. The latter saints did not acknowledge the direct authority of Rome. Instead, they set up a quasi-independent Celtic Church, which consisted of a loose network of monastic foundations. These included centres such as Durrow, Lindisfarne and Kells, each of which contained a scriptorium where illuminated manuscripts were made. Papal authority over the Celtic church was eventually established at the Synod of Whitby in 664 but, by this time, the output from the local scriptoria had reached a very high standard and Bibles and other sacred texts were dispatched from Rome to be copied there.

This historical background of manuscript illumination is important, as it accounts for the types of manuscripts that were produced and also for the highly eclectic nature of their illustrations. Because the Church was still primarily concerned with gaining new converts, the main priority was for books that could be used in missionary work. Accordingly, the greatest achievements of Celtic illumination are to be found in a series of lavish Gospel books. The most famous examples are the Book of Durrow (c. 675), the Lindisfarne Gospels (c. 698) and the Book of Kells (c. 800). The precise format of the Gospel books varied considerably but, in general, they consisted of the first four books of the New Testament, accompanied by three distinctive forms of illustration – portraits of the Evangelists, Carpet-pages and Initial-pages.

The portraits are the least Celtic aspect of the Gospel Books, often reflecting the influence of the manuscripts sent from Rome. Thus, the Evangelists in the Lindisfarne Gospels were closely based on classical models, while the Virgin in the Book of Kells shows strong affinities with a Byzantine icon. These elements contrast sharply with the florid stylizations in the other illustrations.

Carpet-pages were purely ornamental, and usually featured a cross at the centre of the design. More decorative still were the Initial-pages with their extravagant calligraphy, although these also served a practical purpose. The chapter-and-verse divisions of the Bible had not yet been devised, so the huge initials helped the monks to find their way around the continuous blocks of text. In both these cases, illuminators drew inspiration from designs that had figured on earlier Celtic weapons, jewellery and horse-trappings. The designs included intricate, abstract patterns, such as tightly-meshed spirals and interlacing, and an inventive array of fabulous animals, birds and serpents. The creatures were often displayed in ferocious poses, biting their neighbour's tail or coiling around their neck, in a way that can appear ill-suited to their Biblical context. Nevertheless, it is this unique blend of pagan savagery and Christian piety which lends Celtic illumination its potent appeal.

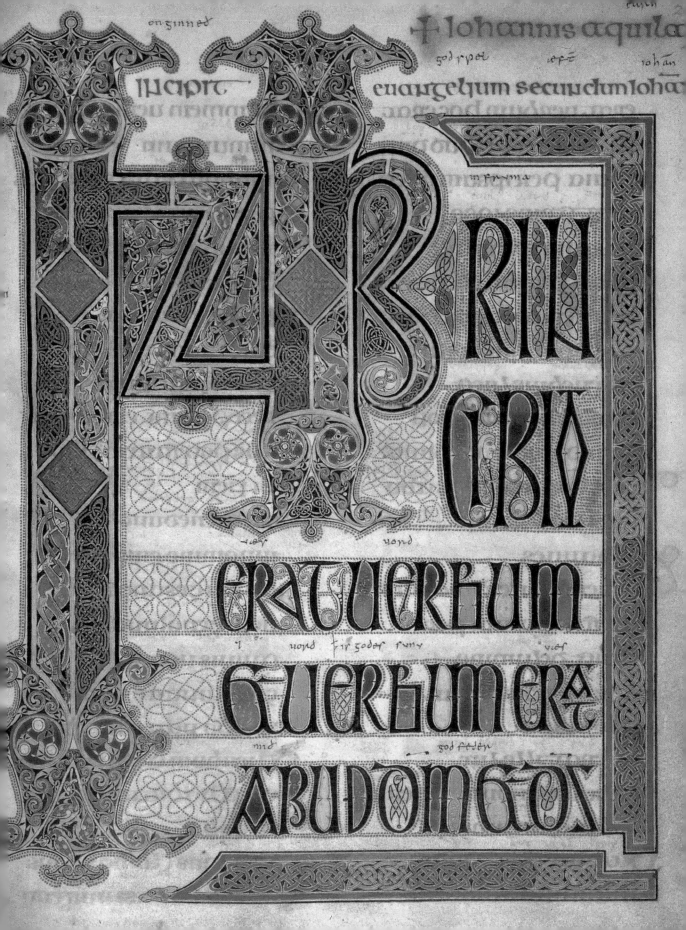

INCIPIT
evangelium secundum Iohan

✝ Iohannis aquila

IN PRINCIPIO ERAT VERBUM ET VERBUM ERAT ABUDOMGOX

WALES

I N THE EARLY Middle Ages, invading Saxons swept into Britain, pressing the Celts into the extremes of the mainland. Throughout this troubled period, the Welsh saw themselves as defenders of the west, the Celtic heroes who might rise one day to hurl the foreign oppressors back into the sea. Hemmed into a beautiful, mountainous country, their political isolation only strengthened their cultural identity. This was still a Celtic nation; a land of bards and druids, where Taliesin composed his riddling verses and King Arthur lay sleeping with his knights, waiting to return.

THE MABINOGION

THE MABINOGION IS a collection of early Welsh tales, which date back to the Middle Ages. They were preserved in two manuscripts, *The White Book of Rhydderch* (c. 1300-25) and *The Red Book of Hergest* (c. 1400). The stories themselves are considerably older. They were probably composed in the eleventh century, and the tale of Culhwch may be earlier still. Individual stories were translated into English from 1795, but the first full translation of the collection was by Lady Charlotte Guest. They appeared in three volumes, between 1838 and 1849. Lady Guest divided the book into three sections: the Four Branches of the Mabinogi (which includes the story of Pwyll), the Four Independent Native Tales (which includes Culhwch), and the Three Romances (which includes Peredur). She added the story of Taliesin from a later manuscript.

THE PLOTS

The three stories narrated here represent the central theme of a quest. In 'How Culhwch Won Olwen', King Arthur's cousin, Culhwch, seeks the hand of Olwen, the beautiful daughter of the giant Ysbaddaden. Before he can win her, he must accomplish many superhuman tasks chosen by Olwen's father. These 'labours' involve Culhwch in magical adventures, often accompanied by King Arthur. The final, and most difficult task, is to catch a magical and ferocious boar and retrieve a comb and razor from between its ears.

In 'Pwyll Encounters Rhiannon', the smitten hero pursues the supernatural horsewoman Rhiannon, and gets involved in a journey that becomes a perilous quest to win her hand.

'Peredur, Son of Evrawc' describes the knight's quest for combat on behalf of King Arthur; but only by submitting to a series of fantastical challenges will he obtain his goal.

THE CHARACTERS

Culhwch Cousin of King Arthur who must hunt the magical boar, Twrch Trwyth, before he can marry Olwen.

Olwen Daughter of the giant Ysbaddaden and suitor to Culhwch.

Ysbaddaden The King of Giants and the father of Olwen, who sets Culhwch the challenge of the Twrch Trwyth.

Twrch Trwyth Supernatural boar hunted by Culhwch, as part of his quest for Olwen's hand.

Arawn King of Annwn, the Welsh Otherworld, who challenges Pwyll to kill his rival, Hafgan.

Pwyll Lord of Dyfed, who becomes Lord of the Otherworld.

Rhiannon Pwyll's supernatural suitor. A goddess associated with Epona (see page 59).

Gwawl Pwyll's rival, betrothed to Rhiannon.

Peredur A questing knight, who undertakes many adventures on behalf of King Arthur.

HOW CULHWCH
WON OLWEN

FTER THE MARRIAGE OF Kilydd, the son of Prince Kelyddon, and Goleuddydd, the daughter of Prince Anlawdd, the Prince's subjects prayed for a son and heir, and their wish was soon granted. Once she became pregnant, however, Goleuddydd lost her reason. For several months she lived in the countryside, refusing to go inside any house. Then, as her delivery time drew near, she regained her senses and took shelter in the dwelling-place of a local swineherd. But Goleuddydd was afraid of pigs and the sight of them hastened the birth. Because of this, the boy was given the name Culhwch or 'Pig-run', after the place where he was born. Yet in spite of this ignoble beginning, the boy was of noble lineage, a first cousin to Arthur, so they took him to be raised at court.

Not long after the birth, Goleuddydd fell ill and called her husband to her. 'I shall die of this sickness,' she said, 'and you will want to take another wife. That is quite natural but, even so, you must do all in your power to protect the rights of your firstborn. I ask you, therefore, not to take a new wife until you see a briar with two blossoms upon my grave.' She also asked him to tend her grave each year, so that it would not become overgrown too quickly. After her death, Kilydd was true to his word and, for seven years, nothing grew on her grave. Only after all this time did he neglect the promise he had made to her.

Then, one day, the king passed the burial place when he was out hunting, and he noticed a briar growing on Goleuddydd's grave. At once, he consulted with his counsellors about finding a new bride. One of them suggested the wife of King Doged, and this idea found favour with Kilydd. So, a force of warriors was sent out and they killed Doged, pillaged his land, and carried off his wife and daughter. Kilydd took the widow as his queen but, remembering his promise to Goleuddydd, he told her nothing of Culhwch's existence.

Now the new queen was anxious to learn more about the man who had taken her from her husband. Shortly after the wedding, she visited a toothless crone, who was known to have the power of divining. The hag told her about Culhwch and she then confronted the king. Kilydd could no longer lie about his son and, reluctantly, he sent messengers to bring him to the court.

Culhwch was well received by his stepmother. She praised his youthful good looks, saying: 'You would do well to take a wife, young prince. I have a daughter who has been wooed by many a noble suitor. You shall meet her and take her as your bride.'

But the youth blushed deeply at the idea. 'I am not yet old enough to marry,' he said quietly.

This reply angered the queen, who took it as a snub and answered. 'If that is how you feel, then I will tell you your destiny. I swear to you, that you will never know the touch of a woman until you win the hand of Olwen, the daughter of the giant Ysbaddaden Pencawr.'

Culhwch then went to his father to report this prophecy. He evidently knew little of Ysbaddaden's fearsome reputation, for he said: 'That will not be difficult, my son. Go to your cousin Arthur and ask him to arrange it for you.'

The youth set out for Arthur's court. He was richly apparelled in a purple mantle with golden trimmings, and there was gold in his boots and stirrups to the value of three hundred cattle. In his hand, he carried two silver spears and, at his side, there was an ivory war-horn and a glittering sword inlaid with gold. Two white-breasted greyhounds ran before him and, in their collars, there were rubies that would have been the envy of many a young maid.

Arthur greeted his cousin warmly, offering him the hospitality of his court. But Culhwch was anxious to begin his quest, and asked his kinsman if he could help him secure the hand of Olwen.

'I have never heard of the girl,' replied Arthur, 'but I will gladly send out messengers to see if she can be traced.' So Culhwch remained at the court until the end of the year. After this time, the messengers returned, only to report that their search had proved fruitless. Culhwch was filled with impatience at this news, vowing to go and seek out the maid himself. But Arthur's companions held him back, chiding him for his impatience.

'Let us come with you,' said Kai, rising from his seat. 'We will not part company from you until you win her, or until you accept that she does not exist.' Kai's offer of help was invaluable, for his powers made him a formidable ally. He could hold his breath under water for nine days and nine nights, and he could go without sleep for the same amount of time. No physician could heal a wound made by his sword. When he wished it, he could make himself as tall as a tree, and he also had the power to generate heat. Whatever he carried during a rainstorm would remain perfectly dry; so dry that it could even be used to light a fire.

Arthur called on several other warriors to accompany Culhwch. First, there was Bedwyr. No one in the land could equal him for speed except Arthur and Drych Ail Kibdar. And, even though he was one-handed, he was as deadly on the field of battle as three ordinary men. Opponents also feared Bedwyr's lance, for it could produce a wound that was nine times larger than a normal spear.

Then Arthur summoned Kynddelig the Guide, who knew all the countries around his domains, and Gwrhyr Gwalstawt, who spoke many languages. Next, he called upon his nephew, Gwalchmai, who had been on many perilous quests, and Menw, the son of Teirgwaedd, who was skilled in the art of casting charms and illusions. So, when all the due preparations had been made, the party left Arthur's court and journeyed out to a vast, open plain. Here, they espied a marvellous castle, the finest that any of them had ever seen. They travelled for three long days before they finally reached it. As they drew close, they came upon an enormous flock of sheep, that stretched as far as the eye could see. No one dared to steal them from the herdsman, because when he was angry, flames poured out of his mouth. All around him were trees and bushes that had been charred by his fiery breath.

Bravely, Kai and Gwrhyr approached him. 'Who owns the castle and these sheep?' they enquired.

'Are you fools?' he snapped. 'Surely everyone knows that they belong to Ysbaddaden Pencawr. Anyway, who are you to ask such questions and what are you doing here?'

'We have come from Arthur's court to seek the hand of Olwen for one of our companions.'

Now the herdsman's tone turned dramatically from anger to pity. 'If you have any sense, you will forget that. None of the men who have come here on such a quest have ever left alive.'

Culhwch thanked him for his information and made him a present of a golden ring. The herdsman tried to put it on, but it was too small for him, so he slipped it onto the finger of a glove instead. Then he took it home and offered it to his wife. 'Where did you get this?' she asked.

'I went fishing by the sea and I found a corpse washed in by the tide. It was the body of a woman, the most beautiful I have ever seen. This ring was on one of her fingers, so I thought I would peel it off and bring it to you.'

'Oh you teller of tales!' exclaimed his wife. 'The sea strips the dead of all their jewels. Show me this bountiful corpse.'

Then the herdsman told his wife the truth, how Culhwch had given him the ring and how he and his companions were coming to share their hospitality that evening. A little while later, they arrived and the woman served them well with food and drink. Afterwards, while everyone was busying themselves with preparations for the following day, she opened up a stone chest by the hearth and out sprang a golden-haired youth.

'Who is this lad?' asked Gwrhyr, 'and what has he done to be confined like this?'

'He is the last of my sons,' replied the woman sadly. 'Ysbaddaden has already killed twenty-three of my boys, and I have no doubt that this one will go the same way as the others.'

'Then let him come with us,' said Kai. 'He shall not lose his life, unless I lose mine first.'

She pondered for a while, before changing the subject. 'And what brings you to this place, sirs?'

'We have come to seek the hand of Olwen for Culhwch,' they replied.

The woman then gave them the same advice as her husband. 'Go now. Forget your quest and leave this place, before anyone from the castle knows that you are here.'

'We cannot do that without seeing the maid,' said Kai. 'Does she ever venture out of the castle?'

'She does,' the woman admitted. 'She comes here each week to wash her hair. I will send for her, if you like, but only if you promise that you will do her no harm.'

They agreed to this and, at long last, Culhwch was able to feast his eyes on Olwen. She came in a robe of flame-coloured silk, and wore about her neck a golden torc, studded with emeralds and rubies. Her hair was yellower than broom, her skin was whiter than sea-foam, her fingers were more delicate than sprays of wood anemone, and her eyes were as clear as the swiftest falcon. 'Lady,' said Culhwch, 'I have loved you since I first heard your name. Come with me now, I implore you.'

'Sir, that cannot be. I have sworn to my father that I will never leave without his consent, for he must die on the day that I wed. I can give you some advice, however, should you wish it. Go to my father and ask him what he will accept in exchange for my hand. If you bring him what he wants, you shall have me; if you fail, you will never escape with your lives.'

Undaunted by this prospect, Culhwch and his companions headed for the castle. There, they slew the nine gatekeepers and the nine watchdogs, that were guarding the place, and marched forward into the hall.

'Greetings, Ysbaddaden Pencawr,' they cried, 'we have come here to ask for the hand of your daughter Olwen.'

The giant raised his enormous head. 'Where are my pages and servants?' he called out. 'Let them bring forks to prop up my eyebrows, which have fallen over my eyes. For I want to observe this so-called son-in-law.' The forks were put in place, and Ysbaddaden stared at Culhwch and the group for a while. 'Come again tomorrow and you shall have my answer,' he said gruffly.

They rose to go but, suddenly, Ysbaddaden seized a poisoned spear and hurled it at them. Bedwyr caught it and flung it back at the giant, wounding him in the knee. 'My curses on you,' he yelled. 'This stings like the bite of a gadfly and now I shall be lame until the end of my days.'

The warriors returned again on the next two days and, both times, Ysbaddaden tried to attack them but without success. Eventually, he relented and presented Culhwch with a long list of tasks that he must perform. There were thirty-nine of these in all, and many revolved around the hunting of Twrch Trwyth, a king who had been turned into a boar.

'In all the world,' said the giant, 'there is neither a comb nor a set of shears that can help me manage my tangled hair, apart from those that are to be found between the ears of Twrch Trwyth, the son of Prince Taredd. Know that he will never give them to you freely, and that you will not succeed in taking them from him.'

'It will be easy for me to do this task, although you may think otherwise,' replied Culhwch.

'Even if you manage this, there is another thing that you may not get,' continued Ysbaddaden.

'No one can hunt the boar without the leash of the hound Drudwyn, the pup of Greid. This leash must be made from the beard of Dillus Varvawc. And this will be useless, unless the hairs of Dillus's beard are plucked while he is still alive. For the beard of a dead man would prove too brittle.'

'It will be easy for me to get this, although you may think otherwise,' replied Culhwch.

'Though you get this, there is another thing that you may not get. There is no finer huntsman in the land than Mabon, the son of Modron. He was stolen from his mother when he was just three nights old and no one knows his present whereabouts. Indeed, no one knows whether he is alive or dead.'

'It will be easy for me to find him, although you may think otherwise,' the prince replied.

'Even if you manage this, there is another thing that you may not get. Mabon cannot be found, unless you first locate his cousin Eiddoel, the son of Aer.'

'It will be easy for me to do this, although you may think otherwise,' repeated Culhwch.

TORCS

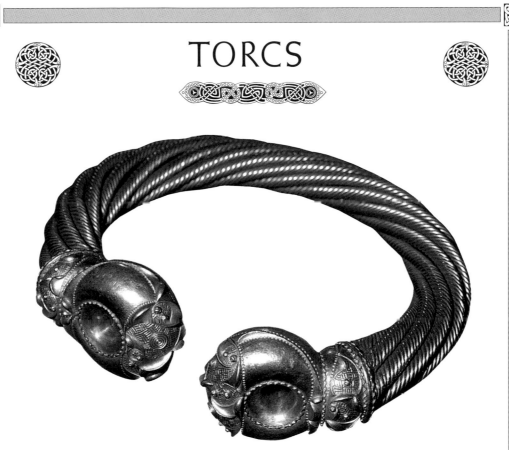

The Snettisham Torc. Torcs indicated high social status and were also closely associated with Celtic deities.

Torcs were decorative neck-rings. Early examples date back to the Hallstatt era, demonstrated by lavish finds at the burial site of Hochdorf in Germany, a Celtic settlement thought to have existed from the sixth century BC. The practice of wearing torcs appears to have come from the East and, initially, they were more common in female graves. Later, they were linked almost exclusively with men.

Torcs indicated high rank and status. Often made of gold, chieftains were often buried wearing them. They were also used as votive offerings, sometimes suffering ritual damage.

At Tayac in Gaul, for example, a torc was split into three and buried with a hoard of coins. The presence of a torc could indicate divinity. Celtic gods were often shown wearing one torc and holding a second, symbolizing abundance.

Torcs were mentioned in a number of literary and historical sources. In *The Mabinogion*, Olwen wore a jewelled torc, while Dio Cassius claimed that Queen Boadicea always donned 'a great twisted golden necklace' before she went into battle. The fact that there have been several major finds of torcs in her tribal area tends to suggest that this claim was accurate.

'Though you get this, there is another thing that you may not get,' said the giant. 'If you are to wed my daughter, you need a cauldron for the wedding feast. The only one that will suffice belongs to Diwrnach, the steward of Prince Odgar, and he will never let you have it without a fight.'

'It will be easy for me to do this, although you may think otherwise.'

'Even if you get this, there is another thing you may not do. Before my daughter weds, my head must be washed and my beard shaved. I will not allow this unless you have bested the great boar.'

'It will be easy for me to manage this, although you may think otherwise,' replied Culhwch.

'Go then. If you can achieve all these wonders, you shall have my daughter for your wife.'

The company journeyed back together to Arthur's court, and he and his warriors joined in the search for the many items that Ysbaddaden had listed. One such expedition brought them to the Castle of Glivi, where Eiddoel was imprisoned. Glivi was alarmed when he saw the force gathered at his gates, and he called down to Arthur from the ramparts.

'What is it you want? There are no riches here, nor any great store of grain.'

'I mean you no harm,' Arthur replied, 'but I ask for the prisoner that is in your care.'

'You shall have him,' said Glivi, 'although I do not want to surrender him.'

So, Eiddoel was then added to the party. And Arthur sent him with a group of his warriors to see the bird known as the Ousel of Kilgwri. Gwrhyr the Interpreter addressed him: 'Tell us if you know anything of Mabon, the son of Modron, who was taken from his mother's bed when he was three nights old.'

'When I first came here,' answered the Ousel, 'I was a very young bird. There was a smith's anvil in this place and, since my arrival, no one has touched it apart from myself. Now, with just the pecking of my beak, I have reduced it to a few scraps of metal. And I promise you that, in all that time, I have never heard of the man you mention. Even so, I will help you. There is a race of animals that was created before me, and I will guide you to their leader.'

The Ousel brought them to the Stag of Redynvre, and Gwrhyr spoke again: 'Oh gracious Stag, we have come to you on a mission from Arthur, as we know of no animal older than you. Tell us if you have heard anything of Mabon, the son of Modron, who was stolen from his mother's bed.'

The Stag tossed his head. 'When I first came to this place, it was an open plain. Not a tree could be found on it, apart from a single sapling. That sapling grew into a mighty oak with a hundred branches, and now it has perished, leaving nothing behind but a withered stump. Yet, in all that time, I can truly say that I have never heard of this Mabon. Since you come from Arthur, however, I will do my best to assist you. I will lead you to a creature that is even older than I.'

The Stag was as good as his word, ushering them swiftly into the presence of the Owl of Cwm Cawlwyd. Then he spoke to the owl on their behalf: 'Owl of Cwm

Cawlwyd, I bring you a mission from Arthur. Can you tell them anything of Mabon, the son of Modron, who was seized from his mother?'

'If I knew anything,' said the Owl, 'you can be sure I would tell you. For I am almost as old as this valley. When I first came here, it was a densely wooded glen. But a race of men arrived and uprooted it. Then a second wood grew in its place, and the forest you see before you now is the third. Even so, in all this time, I have heard nothing of the man you seek. Still, let me try to help you. I will take you to meet the oldest and most widely-travelled creature in the whole world.'

So now Arthur's men were taken to see the Eagle of Gwern Abwy. Gwrhyr repeated his question about Mabon, and the Eagle gazed on him with a long, cool stare. 'I have been here for many an age,' said the Eagle. 'When I first arrived, there was a great boulder here, and I used to perch on it each evening and peck at the stars. Over the years, that rock has worn away and now it is nothing more than a pebble. Yet, in all that time, I have only heard the name of Mabon mentioned once. It happened, one time, when I had strayed as far as Llyn Llyw in search of food. There, I came upon a fat salmon and I dug my talons into it, thinking it would serve to feed me for many a meal. But the salmon was very powerful. It dragged me down into the waters and I was lucky to escape with my life. Angered at this, I summoned others of my kind to help me attack and destroy the fish. The salmon sent messengers, however, and made peace with me, and we have become such firm friends that I have pulled some fifty fish hooks out of his back. Come with me now, for I believe he may be able to help you.'

Arthur's men followed the Eagle until they came to a gushing torrent. Then the bird called out: 'Salmon of Llyn Llyw, I have brought a questing party to speak with you. They come from Arthur and they seek a man named Mabon, son of Modron.'

The Salmon appeared on the water's surface and replied: 'I will tell you as much as I know. With every tide, I travel upstream as far as the walls of Gloucester. There, I have found so much wickedness, that it would amaze you. I will prove it. Let two of you climb upon my shoulders, and I will swim there now.'

So Kai and Gwrhyr clambered upon the Salmon's back and they set off for Gloucester. At length, they came to the walls of a prison, where they could hear loud wails and cries.

'Who makes such a wailing in this house of stone?' asked Gwrhyr.

'It is I, Mabon, the son of Modron,' came the cry from within, 'and never was any man imprisoned more unjustly than I.'

'Can your freedom be purchased with gold or silver,' asked Arthur's men, 'or can it only be bought with a bloody battle?'

'Fighting, alone, can secure my release,' said the prisoner.

The company returned to Arthur with this news, and he immediately raised an army and brought it to the walls of Gloucester. There, they launched a frontal attack on the castle, while Kai and Bedwyr rode to the prison on the Salmon's shoulders. Then, breaking down the walls of the dungeon, they rescued Mabon, and carried him away on the Salmon's back.

Not long after, Kai and Bedwyr climbed the beacon at the top of Plinlimmon, while a fierce wind gusted violently

CAULDRONS

A bronze cauldron found in Llynfawr, Wales.

CAULDRONS PLAYED an important part in the everyday lives of many prehistoric peoples. Archaeological remains from the end of the Bronze Age have demonstrated that they were employed at ceremonial feasts and in certain funerary rites. During the Celtic era, cauldrons were also used in votive offerings at holy sites. Sometimes, they were crammed with valuable objects while, in other cases, the cauldron itself constituted the offering. Celebrated examples have been recovered from peat bogs in Denmark and northern Germany.

The cauldrons described in Celtic literature and folklore often had magical properties. In one story, for example, King Arthur and his followers travelled to the underworld to steal a fabulous cauldron, which could only be heated by the breath of nine virgins and would never cook food for a coward. Some authorities regard this as an early variant of the quest for the Holy Grail. The Cauldron of Inspiration and Science in *The Book of Taliesin* is equally magical, and it appears to be an ancestor of the traditional witch's cauldron. The term was also adopted by some Christian authors, however, and there are a number of medieval poems that describe the Virgin Mary as a 'cauldron of inspiration'. In addition, cauldrons were associated with death and regeneration. Therefore, in one tale recounted in *The Mabinogion*, any dead warriors that were cooked overnight in the Cauldron of Bran the Blessed were restored to life, although they lost the power of speech in the process.

about them. From this vantage point, they noticed a billowing cloud of smoke to the south, which did not seem to be affected by the wind. 'This must be a fire lit by some raiding party,' cried Kai, and the two men hurried towards it. As they drew nearer, however, they could see that the smoke came from Dillus Varvawc, who was busy singeing a wild boar.

'There is the greatest villian to escape Arthur's clutches,' said Bedwyr. 'Do you know him?'

'I do, indeed,' replied Kai, 'and what is more I recall that we need him for our quest. We must obtain the hairs of his beard to make the leash of the hound, Drudwyn.'

'How will we manage this,' mused Bedwyr, 'for he will not allow us to pluck his beard freely?'

'Let him guzzle this boar,' said Kai. 'He may then fall asleep, and we will fall upon him.'

They followed this plan, making a pair of wooden tweezers while Dillus was gorging himself. Then, when the brute had finally gone to sleep, Kai dug a deep trench right next to him. When it was ready, they struck Dillus on the head and pushed him into the trench. While he was stuck there, unable to climb out, Kai and Bedwyr plucked every hair from his chin with the wooden tweezers. Only then did they kill the man.

Soon, Arthur's men were ready to go after the great boar, Twrch Trwyth. Arthur was in Cornwall at the time, and he sent out Menw the shape-shifter, to make sure that the comb and shears were still in place between the boar's ears. For, he knew that there was little point in confronting the beast if they had disappeared. Obediently, Menw set about his task. News had reached him that the boar was in Ireland, where he had ravaged a third of the countryside. So Menw followed him there, eventually catching up with him at Ysgeir Oervel. Then he took the shape of a bird and settled on the roof of the beast's lair, hoping to snatch away one of the precious objects by stealth. When the boar emerged, Menw swooped down, but the only thing that he managed to pluck was one of its bristles. Twrch Trwyth reared up angrily at this affront, shaking himself violently. In the process, some of his venom fell on to Menw's feathers and, from that day onwards, his powers were sorely diminished.

After this, Arthur sent out a messenger to Odgar, an Irish Prince, asking him for the cauldron of his steward, Diwrnach. Odgar agreed to the request and commanded his steward to hand it over. But Diwrnach refused, saying: 'Even if he only wanted to look at my cauldron, I would never allow it.' Arthur's messengers returned with these tidings and, immediately, he assembled a raiding party and sailed across to Ireland in his ship, Prydwen. Diwrnach was alarmed when he saw the strength of this force, so he gave them food and drink in an attempt to appease them. When they had eaten their fill, Arthur turned to his host and demanded the cauldron. But the steward still remained stubborn: 'If I was going to surrender it, I would have given it up at Odgar's command.'

This enraged Bedwyr, who rose from his place and seized the disputed cauldron. Swiftly, he placed it on the back of Hygwyd, the servant who always took charge of Arthur's cooking vessels. The squabble soon led to violence and, in the end, Diwrnach and his entire household were slain. Then Irish warriors then descended on the group, intent on gaining revenge. But Arthur and his men put them to flight and returned to the ship, carrying away a cauldron full of Irish money. They returned with it to Porth Kerddin in Dyfed. And, ever since that time, the place has been known as Messur y Peir or 'the Measure of the Cauldron.'

Then Arthur summoned to his side all the warriors that were in the three offshore islands of Britain: Armorica, Normandy and the Summer Country. With all of these, he travelled across to Ireland. His coming was a source of great fear in that land, so they sent their saints to meet with him and seek his protection. Arthur granted this willingly and, with great relief, the men of Ireland offered him provisions.

Arthur now advanced with his men to Ysgeir Oervel, for it was here that Twrch Trwyth resided with his seven young pigs. Then all the dogs were set loose and the Irish men harried the boar, causing a great commotion. But the boar retaliated furiously, creating havoc throughout a fifth part of Ireland. Next day, Arthur's men took up the fight, but they fared no better than the Irish, receiving only wounds and sores for their troubles. On the third day, Arthur himself did battle with Twrch Trwyth. And this encounter lasted for nine days and nine nights. At the end of it, he had achieved nothing, not even the death of a single piglet. And all who witnessed this were amazed at the ferocity of the beast, wondering how he came to be so vicious. So Arthur explained that the creature had once been a king, until God turned him into a swine to punish him for his sins.

Arthur then sent Gwrhyr the Interpreter to negotiate with Twrch Trwyth. Gwrhyr took on the shape of a bird and flew to the lair, where Twrch Trwyth was staying with his seven pigs. 'For the sake of He who made you thus,' he said, 'I beseech one of you to come with me to talk to Arthur.'

At this, Grugyn Gwrych, a young boar with silver-coloured bristles, emerged from his shelter and looked at the bird. 'By the power that made us so, we refuse your offer. It is bad enough that we have been transformed into these terrible shapes, without being hunted down by your warriors.'

'Let me reassure you,' said Gwrhyr, 'We have only come for the comb and shears, that are between the ears of Twrch Trwyth. 'Give us these and we will happily leave you in peace.'

'Never,' replied Grugyn. 'The only way you may obtain those precious things is by killing us. And, since you will not leave us alone, I promise you that we will head towards Arthur's lands tomorrow to do all the mischief we can.'

So, next day, the boar and his young ones set out across the sea to Wales. Arthur and his men returned to Prydwen and sailed home, hoping to catch up with the boars before they did too much damage. But when they arrived Twrch Trwyth had already ravaged part of the countryside, killing all the men and cattle who crossed his path. At Cwm Kerwyn, he slew four of Arthur's champions: Gwarthegydd, the son of Kaw; Tarawc, who hailed from Allt Clwyd; Rheidwn, the son of Eli Atver; and Iscovael Hael. Then, the next time he was caught, the beast killed three more men, although he himself was wounded in the process. After this rampage, the boar went into hiding.

It did not take too long to find him. Arthur set his entire pack of hounds on two of the piglets, Grugyn and Llwydawg, and Twrch Trwyth soon emerged to come to their assistance. Arthur and his companions pursued him hotly after this, chasing him through all of southern Wales, as far as the Severn estuary. There, they set on the boar again, driving him into the river. For a moment, Twrch Trwyth was overcome by the water and, as he struggled, two of Arthur's men rode by him on their steeds. Mabon, the son of Modron, came on one side and snatched up the comb, while Kyledyr Wyllt passed by the other side, swiftly grabbing the shears. The boar pressed on towards the sea and disappeared.

Once all the giant's demands had been met, Culhwch ventured back to Ysbaddaden's castle, in company with the herdsman's son and all the others who had grievances against him. They laid before him all the precious objects he had specified. Then Kaw of Scotland stepped up to shave the giant from ear to ear, stripping off the beard and skin until the jawbone itself was visible.

'Are you shaved now?' asked Culhwch.

'I am shaved,' replied Ysbaddaden

'And is your daughter mine now?' enquired Culhwch.

'She is, although you need not thank me for the gift of her. For it is Arthur who has accomplished all the tasks I set you. I would never have given her of my own free will for, with her betrothal, I must forfeit my life to you.'

Then Goreu, the son of the herdsman, seized the giant by his hair and dragged him off to the mound. There, he cut off his head and placed it on a stake, so that all might see it. After this, they took possession of the castle and all of Ysbaddaden's treasure.

That night, Culhwch took Olwen for his bride, and they remained happily together until they died. And all of Arthur's companions dispersed, each man returning to his own home.

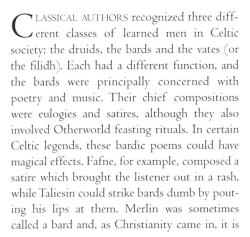

BARDS

CLASSICAL AUTHORS recognized three different classes of learned men in Celtic society: the druids, the bards and the vates (or the filidh). Each had a different function, and the bards were principally concerned with poetry and music. Their chief compositions were eulogies and satires, although they also involved Otherworld feasting rituals. In certain Celtic legends, these bardic poems could have magical effects. Fafne, for example, composed a satire which brought the listener out in a rash, while Taliesin could strike bards dumb by pouting his lips at them. Merlin was sometimes called a bard and, as Christianity came in, it is said that he retired to Bardsey (the island of Bards) with nine bardic attendants where he remained in a magical sleep, guarding the Thirteen Treasures of Britain.

Bardic schools survived after the Celtic era, and their existence was given new impetus by the creation of the Eisteddfod. Dating back to 1176 when it was first organized by Rhys, the Justiciar of Deheubarth, this artistic contest places strong emphasis on music and poetry. Similar contests were held during the Middle Ages, and they were revived on a regular basis in 1789. The modern National Eisteddfod Association was founded in 1880.

THE OTHERWORLD

ONE OF THE MOST striking features of early Celtic literature is the constant intercourse between humans and supernatural beings from the Otherworld. Characters with shape-shifting or other magical abilities were accepted without surprise, and quests to recover objects from their shadowy domains were readily undertaken. This Otherworld realm went by several different names, each of which had its own repertoire of legends. In Wales, it was usually called Annwn, the kingdom which is featured in the story about Pwyll. Here, the place does not seem too menacing, but in 'The Spoils of Annwn' – an episode in *The Book of Taliesin* – it proved deadly. Arthur's quest to retrieve a magical cauldron of plenty cost the lives of most of his men. Equally dangerous were the Hounds of Annwn, spectral dogs that flew through the air at night, presaging death or disaster.

In Irish lore, the Otherworld took on more varied forms and was often associated with the strong Celtic belief in the afterlife. In its most idyllic state, it was Tir na Nog, the Land of the Ever-youthful. Here, Oisin came with his lover, Niamh, and stayed for three hundred years. The Otherworld Hostels or Bruidhen were almost as pleasurable. These resembled a kind of Celtic Valhalla, where the emphasis was on feasting, revelry, music and lovemaking. Of these, feasting seems to have taken pride of place, and each Hostel had its own inexhaustible cauldron, where the animals that were eaten one day came back to life on the next. Trouble could arise, however, and one of the best-known stories recounts 'The Destruction of Da Derga's Hostel'.

Access to the Otherworld could be achieved by a number of routes. The Cave of Cruachan, located near Medb's court, was one of the better-known entry points, but mortals sometimes approached it by sailing across a lake and, in at least one story, it was situated under the sea. At the feast of Samhain, spirits and humans moved freely between the supernatural and earthly spheres. Many Celtic heroes undertook adventures at this time, often invloving shape-shifting, in order to enter the Otherworld.

Another aspect of the Otherworld was highlighted in the sidhe. These were the fairy mounds or underground dwelling-places, where the Tuatha Dé Danaan, an early race of divine beings, were driven after their defeat by the invading Milesians. Each god had his own individual sidh, usually inside a small hill or a prehistoric burial mound. The name has survived in the word 'banshee' (a woman of the fairies).

The association with mounds is significant, as it demonstrates the respect that the early Celts had for the ancient burial sites in their territory. It can be no coincidence that two of the most important sidhe were located at Ireland's most famous archaeological landmarks, Newgrange and Tara. Oenghus lived at Brugh na Bóinne – a megalithic complex, which includes Newgrange – and Finn's battle with Aillen was one of the many adventures set at Tara. The supernatural qualities of these mounds was not confined to their interior. In the tale of Pwyll, for example, the encounter with Rhiannon only becomes possible after the hero has sat down on the mysterious Mound of Arberth, which is clearly the Welsh equivalent of a sidh.

PWYLL ENCOUNTERS RHIANNON

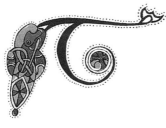HERE WAS NO BETTER spot for hunting than at Glyn Cuch, one of the many domains of Pwyll, the Prince of Dyfed. He rode out there one morning, letting loose his dogs and sounding his horn. But, as he chased after his hounds, he lost sight of his companions. Soon after, he heard the noise of another pack of dogs, running in a different direction. Their cry was very different to that of his own hounds.

Entering a glade, he suddenly spotted the other dogs, pursuing a stag and bringing it down. The colour of these dogs was like no other he had ever seen. Their coats were a brilliant, shining white and their ears were bright red. Pwyll drove them away and set his own dogs on the fallen stag. As he did so, he saw a huntsman riding towards him on a large, dapple-grey steed.

'Chieftain,' cried the newcomer, 'I know who you are, but I will not offer you my greeting. Never have I seen such ignorance and discourtesy.'

'What is the cause of your complaint?' asked Pwyll.

'That kill belonged to me,' replied the other. 'I know of no greater affront than to chase away another man's hounds and set your own in their place. And, though I will not take revenge on you, I will do you more dishonour than if you had stolen a hundred stags.'

'Chieftain,' said Pwyll, 'if I have done you wrong, I will make amends. Tell me who you are and how I may redeem your friendship.'

The other considered for a moment, before replying: 'I am Arawn, King of Annwn, and there is indeed a service that you might do for me. There is a neighbouring king called Hafgan, who is always making war on my domains. If you rid me of his oppression, which is easily within your power, then my friendship shall be yours.'

'Gladly,' said Pwyll. 'Show me how it may be done.'

'This is the way it will happen,' explained Arawn. 'I will put on you my form and looks, and send you to Annwn in my stead. No one in my kingdom – not my wife, my chamberlain, or any other officer – will realize that it is you, and not me who rules there. Then, exactly one year from tomorrow, we shall meet again in this very spot.'

'Very well,' said Pwyll, 'but how am I to deal with this fellow, Hafgan?'

'We have already arranged to meet at the ford, a year from tonight. Go there in my place and give him a single blow. Strike him no more than once, or he will recover all his strength.'

'And what is to happen with my own domains, in the meantime?'

'Fear not,' said Arawn, 'for I will take on your shape, and govern there until we meet again.'

So it was agreed. And Arawn led Pwyll away from that place, and showed him the way to his court. Pwyll walked round it admiringly, for the halls and the chambers and the buildings were the most beautiful he had ever seen. Pages came and helped him off with his hunting gear, and two lackeys brought him a garment of pure, golden silk. Then the court assembled and it seemed to Pwyll the finest and best-equipped one in the world. At its centre was the queen, the fairest woman that he had ever beheld, dressed in a lavish satin robe. Pwyll sat beside her at the banqueting table and, as she began to converse with him, he was struck by her grace and delicacy. 'Surely,' thought Pwyll, as they passed the evening in talking, drinking and eating, 'there can be no better court on earth than this'.

When it was time to sleep, Pwyll joined the queen in her chamber. But, as soon as they were in the bed, he turned his back to her and faced the wall. Throughout the night, he neither spoke to her nor touched her. Yet, the next morning, they resumed their friendly manner towards each other.

This pattern was repeated throughout the entire year. No matter how tender and affectionate Pwyll and the queen might be by day, by night they remained distant.

The year passed pleasantly in hunting, feasting and carousing. Then, all too soon, the night of the meeting with Hafgan came around. Pwyll travelled to the place with his company of knights. The men waited at the water's edge, while he advanced into the ford, to do battle with the opposing king. With his first attack, Pwyll struck a powerful blow that cut Hafgan's shield in two, pierced his strong armour and threw him from his horse. The wounded king moaned, as he lay in the chilling water, 'Oh chieftain, I do not know why you should wish to kill me but, since you have dealt me a deadly blow, take pity and finish me off.'

Now Pwyll remembered the advice of Arawn. 'No, chieftain. I may have regrets about wounding you, but I will not kill you. If anyone else wishes to attack you, they are free to do so, but I will strike no more.'

Hafgan was dismayed at this. 'Loyal followers,' he cried out, 'bear me away, for my death is certain and I can no longer protect you.'

Then Pwyll addressed the knights of the defeated man. 'My lords,' he said, 'take counsel and decide whether or not you are willing to be my subjects.'

'Master, we are,' was the common reply of the men. This was the way in which Pwyll united the two opposing factions in Annwn.

On the following day, Pwyll returned to Glyn Cuch to keep his appointment with Arawn. The two men rejoiced at seeing each other again. 'May heaven reward you for your friendship', said Arawn, 'for I have heard of the

service you have rendered me. What I have done for you, you will discover when you return to your dominions.' Whereupon, he restored Pwyll to his proper state and the two men parted.

Then Arawn took on his own form once more and headed back to Annwn. He had missed his courtiers and companions, and was overjoyed at seeing them again. For their part, however, the day was like any other, since they had known nothing of his absence. Arawn spent the entire day talking and making merry with the queen and his household. Then, when it drew late, he went to bed with his wife. There, he began to caress her lovingly and converse with her. She was confused at this sudden change in his manner and made no response. So Arawn spoke to her a second time, and then a third. 'Why are you so silent?' he asked, at last.

'My lord,' she replied, 'you know full well that, in this past year, we have neither touched nor spoken in our chamber.' Arawn was amazed at this, and explained to her all the details of his pact with Pwyll. And both of them marvelled at the latter's sense of loyalty and honour.

Pwyll, meanwhile, had returned to Dyfed, eager to question his nobles and find out how his kingdom had been ruled during that past year. They praised him sincerely, assuring him that he had never been more wise, more just or more generous. Pwyll rejoiced at this, relating to his companions the full story of the miraculous exchange that had occurred. He promised them, moreover, that he would do his best to govern in the same, just manner as Arawn.

From this time on, there was a strong bond of friendship between these two kings. They sent each other gifts of horses, greyhounds, hawks and many other tokens of goodwill. And, in recognition of the way that he had united the two kingdoms for Arawn, Pwyll was no longer known as Prince of Dyfed. Henceforth, his title was Pwyll, Chief of Annwn.

On another occasion, Pwyll was in his palace at Arberth, feasting with a large assembly of his men. After the first sitting, he arose and went for a walk with a number of companions. Shortly, they came to a place called Gorsedd Arberth or 'the Mound of Arberth'. There was a strange legend attached to this mound, as one of the courtiers explained. Anyone who sat there would either receive wounds and blows, or else would witness a wonder. Pwyll made light of this. 'I hardly think I will receive any wounds or blows while I am with you, my friends, but I would be glad to see a wondrous sight.' And, with this, he went off to sit on the mound.

He had not been there long, when a lady in a golden robe appeared, riding on a snow-white horse. 'My lords,' cried Pwyll, 'do any of you know that lady?' 'No, lord,' they replied. 'In that case,' he continued, 'will one of you go over to her and find out her name?'

Immediately, one of the men arose and walked towards the woman. He showed no great sense of urgency, as her horse only appeared to be moving at a slow canter. Even so, he could not catch up with her. He started to run but, the faster he went, the further ahead she seemed to be. When he realized that the task was hopeless, he returned to Pwyll and told him that no one could follow her on foot.

'Very well,' said the king. 'Go now to the court, take the swiftest horse we have, and follow her.' The fellow did as he was told. He chose the fastest horse in Arberth and galloped after the woman. When he reached open country, he dug his spurs into the animal's side and rode at full speed. Despite this, the horsewoman remained as far away as ever, even though she only seemed to be ambling along at a gentle pace. Soon, the courtier's horse began to tire and he was forced to give up the chase. 'Lord,' he said, 'it is pointless to try and catch that lady. I know of no faster horse in the kingdom than the one I am riding, but it failed me completely.' Pwyll agreed and led them all back to the court, but inwardly he was convinced that there was some trickery in this affair.

Next day, Pwyll and his courtiers enjoyed themselves as before. Then, after they had eaten, Pwyll suggested that they should return to the mound. This time, however, he went prepared. One of his underlings was instructed to bring along a swift steed, so that there should be no delay in setting off after the lady. His foresight was soon rewarded. Not long after they had reached the mound, the horsewoman appeared on the highway, taking the same route as before. On a sign from Pwyll, the youth leaped into his saddle and hurried towards her. But, once again, the lady would not be caught. The lad tried mimicking her gentle pace and he tried giving the horse full rein. Nothing worked. Whatever he did, the distance between them remained the same. At length, he gave up and returned to Pwyll, explaining that the pursuit was hopeless. 'So I see,' said Pwyll, 'but she must have some business in this place, if only she would declare it.'

Pwyll was disappointed, but more determined than ever to unravel the mystery. The next day, therefore, he had a groom prepare his own horse and bring it to the mound. So, when the lady appeared again, as expected, Pwyll mounted up and rode after her. He spurred the horse on, but soon found that his efforts were no more successful than those of the previous two days.

'Lady,' he called out, 'for the sake of the one you love best, wait for me.'

'Gladly,' she replied, 'and it would have been better for your horse if you had made that request earlier.' With these words, she came to a halt and drew back the veil covering her face. She gazed at him and Pwyll knew that, of all the ladies he had ever seen, none could compare with her in beauty.

'Tell me, lady,' he asked, unable to contain his curiosity, 'where are you from and what brings you here?'

'My chief purpose,' she answered, 'was to look for you.'

'I am delighted to hear it,' said Pwyll. 'And will you let me know your name?'

'I will, my lord. I am Rhiannon, daughter of Hefeydd the Old, and I come because I am being given to a man against my will. I have refused him, because of

my love for you, and I will continue to refuse all other offers of marriage, unless you reject me. Will you tell me now, what I should do?'

Pwyll did not hesitate to answer. 'By heaven,' he said, 'if I was offered every woman in the world, it is you that I would choose.'

'If that is so,' she said, 'then make your pledge quickly, before I am given to this other man.'

'The time cannot come soon enough for me,' he assured her. 'Tell me what I must do.'

'Meet me a year hence, at Hefeydd's palace. I will see that a feast is prepared for you, and then you may speak with my father.'

'Let it be so,' said Pwyll. And, with that, the couple parted and he returned to his men. They had a thousand questions about the mysterious lady, but Pwyll told them nothing, immediately changing the subject.

Pwyll kept his secret throughout the year until, at last, the day arrived when he was to travel to Hefeydd's court. He took a hundred knights with him, and they were received with great honour and rejoicing. Pwyll sat between Rhiannon and her father, and a sumptuous feast was brought before him and his men.

They had just finished the first course, when a stranger entered the hall. He was tall, with auburn hair, and he had a regal manner about him. Pwyll beckoned to him to sit down and join their festivities, but the young man declined. 'I cannot,' he said, 'for I have come on an errand.'

'Name it,' said Pwyll.

'It concerns you, my lord. I have come to ask you a favour.'

'If it lies in my power, you shall have whatever you wish.'

At this, Rhiannon groaned.

'Whatever made you say that?'

But the youth still addressed Pwyll. 'You have given me your word in front of all these nobles, have you not?'

'I have. What is it you wish?'

'The lady I love best is to be given to you this night. I have come to ask for her and for her wedding feast.'

Pwyll was silent. 'You do well to say nothing,' complained Rhiannon, 'for I never heard a man utter such foolish promises.'

'I did not know who he was,' Pwyll protested.

She enlightened him. 'This is the man that I was being forced to marry: Gwawl, the son of Clud, a man of great power and wealth. Now, because of your rash words, you will have to give me to him, or you will bring great dishonour upon yourself.'

'Lady, what are you saying? You know I can never agree to this.'

But Rhiannon was firm. 'You must. Give me to him, and I will do whatever I can to rectify the situation.'

'How will you do that?'

'I will give you a small bag,' she said. 'Look after it well and return with it here, on the night of my wedding with Gwawl. On that night, you must come into the hall dressed in ragged clothing. Remember, too, to bring your hundred knights and conceal them in the orchard. The rest I shall explain to you later.'

Gwawl, meanwhile, was growing impatient. 'My lord, I await your answer to my request.' Pwyll turned to him. 'As I have promised, you shall have what is in my power.'

'But,' added Rhiannon, 'that does not include this feast. I have prepared it for the company of Dyfed, and on no account can it be taken away from them. Come here again a year from now, however, and I shall prepare a feast for you and become your bride.'

Both men accepted this ruling and returned to their domains. The year passed. At the end of it, Gwawl came again to the court of Hefeydd the Old, where his arrival was received with great rejoicing. Pwyll, the Chief of Annwn, also came as arranged, waiting in the orchard with his company of a hundred men. He was wearing coarse, ragged clothing and old boots, just as Rhiannon had directed, and there was a hunting horn tied at his waist. He remained outside, until he knew that the first course was over. Then he took up the bag that Rhiannon had given him and made his way into the hall.

'Welcome, sir,' said Gwawl, 'may you be blessed with good fortune and prosperity.'

'Thank you,' replied Pwyll, 'and may fortune reward you also. I come, my lord, to crave a favour.'

'Name it,' said Gwawl, choosing his words carefully, 'and if it is reasonable, I will grant it.'

'It is a small favour and I ask it only out of hunger. Would you fill this bag with food for me?'

'That is reasonable,' agreed Gwawl, 'and it shall be done. Bring him food.'

Upon this order, Gwawl's waiting men arose and began to fetch meat from the banquet. But the bag had a most unnatural capacity. However much food the servants placed inside it, it always remained half-empty.

'What, will this bag of yours never be full?' cried Gwawl.

'It will not, my lord,' said Pwyll. 'It can never be filled, unless a man of property and wealth treads down the food and calls out: 'Enough has been put inside.'

'So be it,' said Gwawl, arising from his place. Immediately, he placed his feet in the top of the bag and began to speak. But, before the words were out of his mouth, Pwyll had pulled the sides of the bag up, over Gwawl's head, and tied a knot at the top. Then, reaching for the horn at his side, he sounded the signal for his knights to come in from the orchard. They overpowered Gwawl's attendants and threw them into prison. Then they began to make sport with the bag. Each man poked it with a staff or with his foot, calling out, 'What is here?' At this, all the others replied, 'a badger.' And this was how the game of Badger in the Bag was invented.

Now the unfortunate Gwawl cried out for mercy. This was granted, on the understanding that he made no attempt to seek revenge. He readily agreed and was allowed to depart. Then the hall was set in order for Pwyll and his companions, and the festivities were resumed. Next day, Pwyll and Rhiannon returned to Arberth as man and wife. There, they were greeted by the chief men and the most noble ladies of the land, and none of these people left the court without receiving some bracelet, ring or other precious gift, in celebration of the great event.

Pwyll and Rhiannon ruled Dyfed happily for the next two years. But, in the third year, there was a murmuring of discontent among the nobles, because the royal couple had as yet produced no heir. They went to Pwyll and urged him to take another, younger wife.

Pwyll calmed their fears. 'We have not been married long, my lords. Grant us another year and if, after that, there is still no heir, then I will accede to your wishes.'

So it was agreed and, before the year was out, Rhiannon gave birth to a son. And, as was the custom, six women were brought in to keep watch over the mother and child that first night. But, as luck would have it, the women all fell asleep before midnight. They awoke just before daybreak and were horrified to find that the child had vanished. Then the women were afraid, fearing that they would be burned alive for failing in their duty. So, while Rhiannon slept on, they hatched a plot. There was in the court a deerhound that had recently produced a litter of pups. They took some of these and killed them. Then they smeared the blood on the face and hands of Rhiannon, and placed the bones before her.

In due course, Rhiannon awoke and was appalled at the grisly sight that met her eyes. But, as she begged her waiting-women to tell her what had happened, they rounded on her sharply.

'Lady,' they cried, 'do not protest your innocence to us. For we have had nothing but buffets and bruises from you, as we tried to rescue the child. Surely, there has never been a more violent woman than you. Have you not this night devoured your own child before our eyes?'

'For pity's sake,' said Rhiannon, 'you know full well the falseness of that accusation. If anyone has forced you to say such things, let me know their names and I will defend you from them.'

TALIESIN

TALIESIN IS A semi-mythical figure, who is said to have been the greatest of the Welsh bards. The very sparse historical information about his life suggests that he lived in the sixth century and was in the service of a British chieftain named Urien Rheged, to whom his poems were dedicated. According to tradition, he was the son of Henwg the Bard, otherwise known as St Henwg of Caerleon-upon-Usk. The latter is said to have travelled to Rome, to ask Constantine to send missionaries to Britain. Taliesin was educated at the bardic school of Cattwg, at Llanveithin in Glamorgan, and is said to have become one of the three Baptismal Bards of Britain. He died at Bangor Teivy, and a cairn near Aberystwyth is thought to mark his burial place.

The real fame of Taliesin rests upon the colourful legends that became attached to him in medieval romances. Guest's version of the story places him at Maelgwn's court, but other versions describe him as the Chief Bard of King Arthur or a companion of Bran the Blessed. They also portray him as a prophet, a sorcerer and an initiate of the druidic mysteries. He seems to have been confused with Merlin as their powers were similar and, like Taliesin, Merlin did not have a human father.

'Truly,' they said, 'we would not bring harm on ourselves for anyone's sake.' And, no matter what entreaties she made, Rhiannon could get no better answer out of them.

The horror of this story could not be kept secret. Soon, it reached the ears of Pwyll's nobles and they came to their master, urging him to cast off his wife. But Pwyll refused. He had promised to separate from her if she remained childless, he explained. Since she had given birth to a child, however, he was no longer bound by this obligation. If she had committed a crime, then she should be punished. That would suffice.

The wise men of Dyfed were summoned to decide upon the matter. Rhiannon would not dispute with the women, preferring to accept a penance. So they chose a punishment for her. For a period of seven years, she was to sit near a horse-block at the gate of Arberth. There, she was to relate her story to any stranger, who came to mount or dismount from their horse. She was also to offer to carry them to the court on her back.

Now at that time, the lord of Gwent Ys Coed was Teirnon Twryfliant. Amongst his possessions was a beautiful mare, that foaled every year on the eve of Beltane. But, during the night, the foal always vanished, and no one knew why or what had become of it. Teirnon grew vexed at this and he made a vow that he would sit through the night with the mare, to see what became of its young.

So, on the eve of Beltane, the mare was brought into the house. As usual, the mare gave birth, producing a large and sturdy colt. Teirnon went closer to examine it and, as he did so, he heard a loud commotion. Then a large claw appeared through the window and seized the colt by the mane. Teirnon snatched up his sword and dealt a lusty blow, severing the intruder's arm at the elbow. Swiftly, he rushed outside to see what it was. But the darkness had swallowed the creature up, and he could find no trace of it. When he returned to his house, however, he found an infant boy at his door. The child was wrapped in fine, satin swaddling clothes and looked strong for his age.

Teirnon took the baby inside and showed it to his wife. She marvelled greatly, both at his tale of the night's events and at the sight of the infant. 'What sort of garments are these?' she said, looking closely at the embroidered mantle. 'Truly, he must be the son of some noble folk.' And, because there was no way of knowing who his parents might be, the couple took the child as their own. They called him Gwri Golden Hair, because the few wisps of hair on his head were as yellow as the sun. Then they raised him at court, where everyone was amazed at his prodigious size and strength. He could walk before he was a year old and, by the age of four, he had started nagging the grooms to let him take the horses to water. When Teirnon's wife saw the interest he took in these animals, she persuaded her husband to make him a present of the colt that had been saved on the night they found him. Teirnon readily agreed, and the horse was placed in the care of the grooms, until Gwri was old enough to ride it.

In the meantime, Teirnon had also come to hear about Rhiannon and her punishment. The case was so sad, that he made further enquiries about it, questioning travellers who had been at Pwyll's court. Teirnon had known the Prince of Dyfed in the past and, increasingly, he was troubled by his son's growing resemblance to that lord. Eventually, he went to his wife and shared his fears with her. Together, they agreed that the child should be returned to Pwyll, so that Rhiannon could be released from her cruel and unjust punishment.

The boy was sent back on the following day and his arrival at the court of Dyfed was greeted with much rejoicing. He was given the name Pryderi, and Teirnon was made his foster-father. In the fullness of time, Pryderi succeeded Pwyll as lord of Dyfed.

SACRED WELLS

*Carved relief of three water nymphs from the headstone of a sacred well. Each holds a beaker
and an urn from which the water flows.*

WATER, IN ALL its forms, was revered by
the Celts. Precious objects, such as
ceremonial weapons and jewellery, were frequently thrown into rivers or lakes as votive
offerings. The deliberate discarding of cult
objects in bogs and marshes is probably related
to this. Springs and wells, meanwhile, were
often associated with healing. Here, it was
commonplace for the votive offering to be a
carved wooden figurine, which represented the
limb or organ that needed the cure.

The same sites were also linked with fertility, and believers used to pin small offerings or
'clooties' near the well. In time, the pin itself
became the offering, and there are a number of
Breton shrines where, until comparatively

recently, young women used to place pins in a
figure of the local saint. They did this in the
hope that they would find a husband or con-
ceive a child in the coming year.

Wells also had associations with the
Otherworld and, in Celtic tradition, they often
possessed some magical properties linked to
ritual activity. In many cases, this occurred after
the severed head of an important person had
been deposited in the well. The coming of
Christianity did little to affect the high status
of these sacred sites. The ecclesiastical authorities made great efforts to adapt them to their
own uses and, particularly in Brittany, a holy
well devoted to a local saint can often be found
within the precincts of a church.

PEREDUR, SON OF EVRAWC

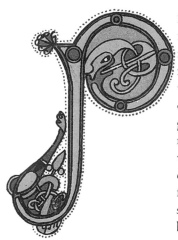

EREDUR WAS THE youngest and only surviving son of Evrawc. His father had owned an earldom in the north and maintained himself not through the wealth of his possessions, but rather by tournaments, combats and fighting. And, as so often happens with men who make war their profession, he ended up losing his life, and six of his sons died alongside him. Peredur was not yet old enough to go off campaigning, and his mother was determined that he should not share the same fate as his brothers. So, she took her son and went to live with him in a remote area. In addition, she chose as her companions only women, boys, and spiritless men, who hated fighting. Under her orders, none of these were allowed to bring swords or armour near the boy. So, most days, he amused himself by throwing holly darts in the forest.

Then, one day, while tending his mother's goats, Peredur spotted two hinds standing close to the animals. He marvelled at these strange-looking goats that had no horns, but ran swiftly after them and drove them into the goat pen near his house. Then he showed his mother what he had done, and both she and her ladies were astonished at this feat.

Another time, not long after this, Peredur saw three knights riding along the horse-track at the edge of the forest. These three were Gwalchmai, the son of Gwyar; Geneir Gwystyl; and Owain, son of Urien. Their trappings caught his eye, so he pointed them out to his mother and asked her what sort of people they might be. 'They are angels, my son,' she replied.

'By my faith,' he thought, 'then I will go and become an angel with them.' So he cut across a field and hurried to catch up with them. The knights, for their part, were pleased to see him, as they were searching for someone. 'Tell me, lad,' asked Owain, 'did you recently see a knight pass by?'

Peredur was baffled. 'I do not know what a knight is,' he replied.

'Someone who looks like me,' said Owain. Then, seeing the boy's interest, he said: 'Look, if you tell me what I need to know, I will tell you about knights.' Whereupon, he began to show him his weapons and armour. At length, when the youth was satisfied, he repeated his question.

'Yes,' said Peredur, 'I have seen the man you are looking for. Go on ahead and I will catch you up, and show you the way.' With that, he hurried back to his mother and blurted out: 'Mother, those were not angels that we saw, but knights.' On hearing these words, the poor woman fainted.

While she was recovering, Peredur ran outside and picked out one of their pack-horses, a bony dapple-grey nag. He strapped some sacking around it, to make a rudimentary saddle, and took some food for the journey. Then he returned to bid farewell to his mother. She was reluctant to let him go but, seeing that he could not be swayed, she gave him some parting advice:

'Go to the court of Arthur, where you will find the boldest and most generous of men. Whenever you pass a church, always stop and say a prayer in it. If you see meat and drink when you are hungry, and no one has the good grace to offer you some, then take it for yourself. If you hear a cry for help, always heed it, especially if it is from a woman. If you see a fine jewel, take it and present it to someone else, for you will gain honour. Finally, if you come across a fair woman, then woo her, whether she wants you to or not, for it will make you more noble.'

After this discourse, Peredur mounted his horse and departed, armed with nothing more than a handful of holly darts. For two days, he traversed the lonely forest without food or drink.

PICTISH SYMBOLS

CELTIC ART displayed some strong regional variations. The Picts, for example, evolved a symbolic language on their stone carvings that has yet to be fully deciphered. More than two hundred of their decorated stone slabs survive, and there must have been many more. The symbols include animals and strange, composite monsters; household objects, such as combs and mirrors; and abstract forms, such as V-shaped rods, Z-shaped rods and crescents.

The slabs themselves may have represented grave markers or territorial boundaries. During the Christian era, the Picts also designed elaborate cross-slabs. On these, the cross was carved in high relief, featuring traditional motifs, while the enigmatic Pictish symbols were confined to the slab's background. Historians have shown a clear stylistic link between Pictish carving and the decorations in some of the illuminated Gospel Books.

At last, he came to a clearing, where he found an elaborate pavilion. He thought it might be a church, so he dismounted from his horse and walked towards it. Inside, he was surprised to find a lovely, auburn-haired girl. She wore a glittering headband, that was set with many jewels, and there was a large gold ring on her right hand. The maid seemed pleased to see Peredur, offering him wine and bread and meat from a wild boar. After he had taken his fill, he came and knelt before her. 'My mother told me that, whenever I saw a fine jewel, I should take it,' he said, looking at her ring.

'With my blessing,' she replied. So Peredur slipped the ring off her finger and went on his way.

Soon afterwards, the knight who owned the pavilion came back to the clearing. Immediately, he saw the tracks leading up to the place. Fearing the worst, he hurried inside and questioned the maiden: 'Tell me, who has been here during my absence?'

'A curious man, my lord,' she replied, describing Peredur's strange manner and behaviour.

'Has he harmed you in any way?' demanded the knight. The girl denied this, but his mind was already made up. 'I don't believe you,' he cried, 'and, until I find him and take my revenge for the wrong he has done me, you won't spend two nights in the same place.' Then he stormed out of the pavilion and rode off to look for the intruder.

Peredur, meanwhile, had journeyed on towards Arthur's court. Shortly before his arrival, a dramatic incident had occurred. An imposing knight strode into the hall, where Arthur and his men were at table. A page was just pouring out some wine for Gwenhwyvar, when the knight snatched the goblet out of his hand and hurled the liquid at the queen's face. Then he fetched her a blow on the head and laid down a challenge to the men of the court. 'If any of you wish to retrieve this goblet and avenge my insult, then follow me to the meadow outside, where I will deal with you.' So saying this, he left to await his combat with their champion.

Inside the hall, however, Arthur's men appeared sheepish. For, it seemed to them, that no man would have the effrontery to commit such a terrible act, unless he had some powerful magic to protect him. It was at this moment, as each knight waited for his neighbour to take up the challenge, that Peredur came into the hall. He made a comical sight on his skinny nag with its mean looking saddle, but he did not feel the least bit self-conscious. Instead, he ambled towards the centre of the hall, still on his horse, and said to Kai: 'Tell me, tall man, which of you is Arthur?'

'Why do you seek him?' asked Kai.

'Because my mother told me to come to Arthur's court and ask him to make me a knight,' replied Peredur.

'Upon my word,' said Kai, 'you have made a curious choice of warhorse and armour.' This comment was greeted with much laughter.

In the midst of all this mockery, a dwarf came forward. He and his wife had been taking refuge in Arthur's court for the past year and, in all that time, neither of them had uttered a word. Now, however, he spoke out in a loud, clear voice: 'Welcome Peredur, son of Evrawc, chief among warriors and a flower of knighthood.'

Kai was scornful of this. 'It shows great ill-breeding, my man, that you have chosen this moment to break your silence, after remaining mute for an entire year, when you might have conversed

LEWIS CHESSMEN

The Lewis Chessmen consists of seventy-eight pieces, hewn from ivory. This expressive
group comprises (left to right) knight, rook, bishop, pawn and queen.

E ARLY CELTIC literature contains frequent references to chess and other, similar board games. In the *Táin*, for example, Cú Chulainn and his friends often played a game called fidchell (literally 'wooden wisdom'), which was said to have been invented by Lugh. In this game, the aim was to move the king to the side of the board, while also blocking the progress of one's opponent.

The Welsh equivalent of the game was called gwyddbwyll. Later, chess provided a colourful feature in many of the medieval romances. In the Castle of Wonders, for instance, Peredur comes across a living chess-board, where the pieces move themselves.

In all the tales, it is clear that these games were luxury objects, used exclusively by the upper classes. The richness of the Lewis Chessmen confirms this; the pieces are made out of walrus ivory and are beautifully decorated. This is especially noticeable in the ornamental panels of the thrones (see opposite).

They were discovered in a sandbank on the Isle of Lewis in 1831, and are thought to date back to the mid-twelfth century. The extraordinary grimaces featured on some of the rooks, or foot-soldiers, with their teeth clamped over the tops of their shields, relates to the antics of the *Táin* fighters, while the pawns resemble the tombs of fallen warriors.

The scale of the pieces suggest that early chess-sets were larger than the average modern equivalent, which makes Diarmaid's marksman-ship (see page 80) slightly more feasible.

DRUIDS

*In early Celtic society, the druid's political and religious
power gave them the highest authority.*

THE DRUIDS played a major role in early Celtic society. In addition to their religious functions, they were judges, teachers and counsellors. Even the High King had to bend before their authority. Thus, in the *Táin*, Sualtam committed a fatal error when he spoke before the druids without permission, although his message concerned a genuine emergency.

Druids were highly secretive about their activities and, as a result, almost all our information comes from classical or Christian sources. Caesar noted that druidic teaching originated in Britain, and that the druids believed in the transmigration of the soul, deciding that this was one of the main reasons why Celtic warriors showed so little fear of death. Along with other classical authors, Caesar dwelt on the gory question of sacrifice. The druids certainly examined the innards of sacrificial animals when divining, but whether they burned humans alive in huge, wickerwork images is more questionable.

The transition to Christianity may have been quite smooth, as some of the early saints had close links with druidism. St Brigid, for example, was raised in a druid household.

with the cream of Arthur's knights.' He then struck the fellow a vicious blow, knocking him out.

Then a female dwarf came forward, echoing the words of her husband. 'Hail Peredur, son of Evrawc, gentlest of knights and beacon of chivalry.' On hearing this, Kai lashed out with his foot and the woman fell to the ground, beside her mate.

'Tall man,' interrupted Peredur, 'I ask you again, which of you is Arthur?'

'Hold your peace,' said Kai. 'First of all, go to the meadow outside and challenge the warrior who is waiting there. Defeat him, seize his goblet, and take his horse and his arms for your own; only then will you be deemed worthy of becoming a knight.'

'Very well,' replied Peredur. Then he rode outside to where the surly knight was waiting.

'Ho there,' cried the fellow, 'did you see anyone coming out to cross swords with me?'

'I was told to come out and take your goblet, horse and armour for myself,' the youth replied.

But the knight was in no mood for joking. 'Enough of such talk, boy. Go back into the court and fetch Arthur or his champion. Tell them to come quickly, or I will not bother to wait.'

'No,' replied Peredur. 'Whether you like it or not, I will have your horse and your armour.'

This enraged the knight and he charged at the lad, striking him a powerful blow on the shoulder with the shaft of his spear. But Peredur just laughed, saying, 'This is not the way I used to play with my mother's servants, but I can easily adapt to your game.' Then he took aim with one of his darts and let fly. It hit the fellow in the eye, passed right through his skull and emerged at the back of his neck, killing him instantly.

Inside the court, meanwhile, Owain was quarrelling with Kai. 'That was a foolish thing to do. The lad will probably be killed or wounded by that warrior, and he will leave with a low opinion of Arthur's knights. I had better go and see what has happened.'

So, Owain went out into the meadow. There, he was amazed to find Peredur tugging at his foe's armour. 'What are you doing?' he called.

'I am trying to strip him of his iron coat but I cannot get it off,' replied Peredur.

'Patience, young man,' said Owain. And he helped the lad undo his enemy's armour and showed him how to put it on. 'There,' he said. 'Now you have some armour and a good horse. Take them, and come with me to see Arthur, for after such bravery he must surely make you a knight.'

But the boy refused. 'Take the goblet back to Gwenhwyvar and assure Arthur that I will always be his subject, and will serve him well. Tell him also, though, that I will never enter his court again, until I have met with the tall man and avenged the injuries he did to the two dwarfs.' And Owain went back inside, and reported to Arthur all that had happened.

Peredur went on his way. He had not gone far, when he met a mounted warrior. 'Where have you come from?' he asked.

'From Arthur's court,' replied Peredur.

'And are you one of Arthur's men?' enquired the warrior.

'Certainly, I am,' the youth replied.

'Then know that I am a sworn enemy of Arthur,' retorted the warrior. 'I kill or maim any of his knights that cross my path.' And, without further ado, the fellow set upon him. Their battle was brief but bloody. Peredur unseated his foe and the villain begged for mercy.

'I will grant you that,' said Peredur, 'provided that you go to Arthur's court and tell him that I have defeated you on his behalf. Say also, that I will not come back until I have avenged the insults made against the two dwarfs.' The man agreed, and immediately carried out Peredur's instructions. Nor was he the last to make his way to Arthur's court with such a message. Within the space of one week, Peredur overcame sixteen other knights, compelling them all to perform the same penance for him. Arthur was greatly impressed by the prowess of this new champion, and rebuked Kai for the folly of his actions.

Peredur's route now led him to a lake, near the edge of a desolate forest. On the far side of the lake, there was a sizeable fortress. Nearer to him, he saw a venerable old man, sitting on a velvet

ISLE OF MAN

THE ISLE OF MAN probably takes its name from an Irish sea god, Manannán Mac Lir. According to tradition, he was the first king of the island. Manannán was a shape-shifter with many magical possessions, such as a boat that obeyed the thoughts of its master and a sword that could penetrate any armour. The horses of his chariot took the form of large waves. His Welsh counterpart was called Manawydan fab Llyr, the subject of a tale in the *Mabinogion*.

Before it fell prey to the Norsemen, the Isle of Man had strong Celtic connections. It had its own language, a dialect of Gaelic, and its now familiar three-legged emblem, the triskele, was widely used in the designs of Celtic craftsmen. The island also shared the same literary heritage. The ballad of Fin as Oshin, for example, is a variant of the Irish story of Finn and Oisin, woven together with anecdotes about King Orry.

cushion at the water's edge. When the man spotted Peredur, he got up and hobbled back towards the castle, for he was lame. Peredur followed him, entering a large hall, where a welcoming fire blazed. He was given food and wine and, when his hunger was satisfied, the old man conversed with him. He asked Peredur if he knew how to wield a sword and made him try out his strength against one of his sons. It proved a simple test, because soon Peredur had cut the lad on the head.

'That's enough,' said the old man. 'Come and sit down now, for I can see that you will become the finest swordsman in this land. You should know that I am your uncle, your mother's brother. Stay with me for a time and I will instruct you in many things; in courtliness and nobility and the customs of other countries. Forget your mother's words, for I will be your teacher from now on. Above all, remember this: if you see something strange, do not ask the meaning of it. If no one has the courtesy to explain it to you, then the blame will fall on me, since I am your tutor.' Peredur willingly agreed to all this and, in due course, he went to his bed.

Next day, he rose at dawn and, with his uncle's permission, rode to the other side of the forest. There, he came upon another castle, similar to that which he had just left. The gate was open, so he entered and proceeded into the hall. Another silver-haired old man awaited him there, surrounded by many friends and attendants. Once more, a lavish meal was laid before Peredur and he was asked if he could use a sword. This time, however, the test was different. The old man handed him a sword and told him to strike a huge iron column. Peredur hit the column and the sword broke in two pieces.

'Now put the pieces next to each other and try to join them,' instructed the old man. Peredur obeyed and, as he did so, the column and the sword became whole again.

'Try once again,' said the ancient. And, as before, the column and the sword split in two, but were mended when Peredur placed the parts together. He struck another blow of similar force, but this time the broken pieces could not be joined together. Peredur looked at the old man but said nothing, remembering his uncle's advice about asking for explanations.

His curiosity was soon satisfied, for his host beckoned to him to sit by him. 'My blessings upon you, lad. You wield that sword as well as any other man. At present, you have two-thirds of your strength. When you have obtained that final third, no one will be able to compete with you. Know, too, that I am your uncle, the brother of the man you stayed with last night.'

Peredur was delighted with this news and he continued talking with his kinsman. While they were conversing, however, he noticed two youths entering the chamber. In their arms, they carried an enormous spear. Three streams of blood trickled from its socket, leaving a crimson trail along the floor. And, when those present in the hall witnessed this sight, they all let out a terrible wail of anguish. Despite the commotion, the old man continued talking to Peredur. A few minutes later, after the clamour had subsided a little, two young girls entered the room. Between them, they carried a large salver. On this, there was a man's head, dripping with blood. The sight of this provoked such a fearful shrieking and sobbing, that Peredur found it painful to remain in the room. But, eventually, the company quietened down and everyone went off to sleep.

Next day, Peredur rose early and, with his uncle's permission, he rode into the forest. Soon he heard a cry and came upon a beautiful, auburn-haired woman, who was struggling to place the body of a man across a saddled horse. But the corpse was too heavy and she could not secure it.

'Tell me, lady,' he said, 'what dreadful thing has happened here?'

'Oh, accursed Peredur,' she cried, 'there's little comfort in seeing you.'

'Why do you call me accursed? How have I offended you?' asked Peredur.

'Because you were the cause of your mother's death. When you rode off against her will, a terrible sorrow gripped her and she died. For that reason alone, you are accursed. In addition, you should know that the dwarfs at Arthur's court were once members of your parents' household. And I am your foster-sister and this is my husband, who has just been slain by the Knight of the Clearing. Hurry away, now, or you may well suffer the same fate.'

Peredur was greatly shocked by this news, but he tried to calm his foster-sister. 'Weep no more,' he said, 'for it does no good. I will bury this man and avenge his death.'

The woman waited while Peredur buried her husband. Then she took him to find the Knight of the Clearing. Peredur soon made short work of the man. After just a few blows, the fellow fell on his knees and begged for mercy.

'I shall spare you,' said Peredur, 'provided that you take this woman in marriage, to replace the husband that you have slain. Then you must go to Arthur's court and tell him that it was I who defeated you, out of service to him.'

The knight agreed and did as he was told. And Arthur and his followers again marvelled at this valiant warrior, lamenting only that he would not join them.

Peredur's wanderings led him into many other perilous adventures. And the strangest of these occurred at the court of the King of Suffering.

After his fight Peredur rode on, until he came to the court of the sons of the King of Suffering. He went inside and was surprised to see only women there. They greeted him joyfully, however, and began to make conversation with him. Then, as they were talking, he noticed a horse arriving with a corpse slung across its saddle. The women left Peredur for a moment, lifted the body off the horse and carried it to a vessel filled with warm water, placed near the door. Putting the body in the water, they washed the corpse, rubbing oils into its skin. As they did so, the man revived. Stepping out of the water, he greeted Peredur warmly. In the meantime, two other horses entered the enclosure, each bearing a corpse, and the women tended them similarly. Seeing Peredur's amazement, the first man explained that, in a nearby cave, lurked a creature known as the Avanc. It killed three of them once a day and, on each occasion, the victims were revived. Because of this, the place was known as the Court of Suffering.

On the next day, the three young men set forth to meet their fate at the cave of the Avanc. Although Peredur was keen to accompany them, they refused him, saying: 'For, if the beast should kill you, you know you have no lady here to revive you.'

Even so, Peredur followed them at a distance. Soon, when they were out of sight, he came to a mound. On this, there sat the fairest maiden that he had ever seen. 'I know your quest,' she said. 'You are going to do battle with the Avanc, but it will kill you, using its cunning rather than its strength. For the creature lives in a cave and, at its entrance, there is a stone pillar. Concealed behind this, the Avanc sees everyone that approaches and swiftly kills them with a poisoned spear. If you promise to love me best of all women, however, I will show you a way to defeat the creature. For I will give you a charmed stone, which will let you see the beast, while you remain invisible.'

'Lady,' said Peredur, 'I loved you the moment I set eyes on you. Tell me where I may find you.'

'When you seek me, look towards India,' she said, then vanished leaving him the charmed stone.

Peredur travelled on, until he came to a river valley. By the bank of the river was a graceful tree. One half was green and leafy, but the other half was aflame. Peredur went past this tree, down the narrow path to the cave. As he drew near, he took the stone in his left hand, gripping his spear in the other. When he entered the place, he saw the Avanc and pierced it with his spear. Then he cut off its head and held it aloft as he emerged. His three companions greeted him, saying that it had been prophesied that he would slay the monster and release them from their sufferings. In reward, they offered him one of their three sisters, and half their possessions. But to each one Peredur replied: 'I did not come here with marriage in mind but, if I had, I think it might have been your sister that I desired the most.'

Then, bidding them farewell, he continued on his way.

LUGHNASADH

LUGHNASADH WAS A summer festival, marking the start of the final quarter of the Celtic year. It was celebrated on August 1 and appears to have been linked to the gathering in of the harvest. This connection was maintained in the Christian feast of Lammas ('loaf-mass'), which superseded it. The pagan festival owes its origins to Lugh, a sun-god whose name means 'the shining one.' According to legend, he established a series of funeral games in honour of his foster-mother, an agricultural goddess called Tailtu, who had died after clearing the forest of Breg. These games were held regularly, along the lines of the early Greek Olympics.

Lugh was worshipped by many Celtic peoples. In Gaul, for example, he was known as Lugus and gave his name to Lyon (Lugdunum). He was also credited with many powers. In Irish tradition, he was revered both as a formidable warrior and a master magician. Lugh aided Cú Chulainn in his struggles against the Connacht forces and helped the craft-gods to forge their magic weapons. Later, his craftsman's role became more emphasized and he was known as Lughchromain ('little stooping Lugh') or, in its anglicized form, the prototype of the leprechaun.

THE BIRTH OF TALIESIN

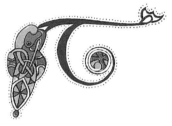

EGID VOEL WAS A man of noble lineage. He lived in Penllyn with his wife Ceridwen. The couple had three children: the firstborn was a good-looking son called Morfran ab Tegid; then came a daughter named Creirwy, the fairest maiden in the world; finally, there was another son, Afagddu, who was as foul to look on as his siblings were fair. And Ceridwen feared that other men of noble birth would exclude him from their society, on account of his ugliness. In the age of King Arthur and his Round Table, the only way to compensate for this, she believed, was to ensure that Afagddu had some special gifts or worthwhile knowledge.

So Ceridwen studied the books of hidden learning, and decided to prepare a cauldron of Inspiration and Science for her son. This would initiate him into the mysteries of the future state of the world and, armed with this knowledge, he would earn the respect of others.

The preparation of the cauldron was long and difficult. It had to boil continuously for a year and a day. Only then, would it produce the three blessed drops of liquor, which would bring divine inspiration to her son. So Ceridwen set Gwion Bach, son of Gwreang of Llanfair, to stir the cauldron and a blind man named Morda to kindle the fire beneath it. And she charged them both that the cauldron was to boil continuously, without a single respite, for the space of a year and a day. She, meanwhile, made herself very busy gathering all manner of charm-bearing herbs. These she then dispensed into the bubbling cauldron at the most propitious moment, when the planets were correctly aligned in the heavens.

Now it happened one day, towards the very end of the year, that Ceridwen was out in the fields collecting plants. During her absence, whilst Gwion Bach was stirring the charmed brew, the three precious droplets meant for Afagddu splashed out of the cauldron and fell onto Gwion's finger. The liquid was so hot that it scalded him, and he instantly began to suck his finger, to cool it. And as he did so, the marvellous potion began to weave its magical spell. From then on, Gwion Bach was blessed with the gift of foresight.

The first thing he perceived with his new powers was that he should beware of Ceridwen, for her skills were varied and powerful. This revelation filled Gwion Bach with utter terror. He knew immediately that he must flee from the house, so he headed back across the fields towards his native land, his fear of her wrath carrying him homewards.

Because the cauldron was left untended, it burst in two and the boiling liquid gushed out from it. This was extremely grave, since all the liquor, with the exception of the three charm-bearing drops, was poisonous. The scalding potion coursed down the hill, forging great furrows in its wake, and gushed into a nearby stream. The water then became poisoned, so when the horses of the nobleman Gwyddno Garanhir drank from it, all of the beasts died. And, from that time on, the stream has been known as the Poison of the Horses of Gwyddno.

Some time later, Ceridwen returned home from her plant-collecting, only to find that her year long toil had been entirely wasted. The cauldron of Inspiration and Science was no more than a molten mass. Full of fear, blind Morda awaited her wrath.

A terrible fury gripped her. She picked up a billet of wood and struck a powerful blow to Morda's head, a blow so forceful that one of his sightless eyes fell out onto his cheek. Piteously, he cried out for mercy. 'You are wrong to disfigure me, mistress, for I am the innocent one. You know that it was not I who wrecked your cauldron.'

'You are right,' said Ceridwen, finally starting to calm down. 'It was not you but Gwion Bach who robbed me of the gift of foresight meant for my son.'

With these words, she set off in swift pursuit of him. But Gwion Bach saw Ceridwen coming after him, and turned himself into a hare, so that he could flee from her more quickly. He raced over hills and valleys, breathless in his efforts to escape her clutches.

Then Ceridwen, not to be outdone, became a greyhound and harried him fiercely. So, he ran to the water's edge, turned himself into a fish and flipped into the depths of the cool water. Still, Ceridwen was without mercy and she transformed herself again. This time she took on the form of a female otter, her sharp teeth waiting to bite the flesh of her quarry. Despite this, Gwion Bach managed to slither away from her once more, making himself a bird of the air. But Ceridwen followed him still.

Now she became a hawk, swooping and gliding, fixing him with her hard eye, giving him no rest in the sky. In desperation, Gwion Bach curled up and wished himself no more than a grain; he dropped into a vast mound of winnowed wheat, lying loose on the floor of a barn. But she was relentless in her pursuit.

Ceridwen changed herself yet again, this time into a crested black hen. In this guise, she scraped the floor of grain until she found him. Then she greedily swallowed him up, whole.

Nine months later, Ceridwen gave birth to a boy child. He was so fair of face that she could not find it in her heart to kill him. Instead, she wrapped him gently in a leather bag and cast him into the sea. The bag swirled around upon the waters for some time, but the infant was not drowned.

By good fortune, the bag holding the boy child was washed into a weir on a beach between Dyfi and Aberystwyth, which belonged to Gwyddno. One year, Gwyddno had promised his son, Elphin, that he could have all the fish he found in the weir; and by selling the fish he could hope to pay his debts.

Elphin happened to be fishing that day. He spotted the leather bag, caught on a pole of the weir, and hooked it out. Greedily, he tore open the wrapping, hoping to find some golden treasure, and was astounded when he discovered a baby boy inside. He carried him to his horse, and placed him gently in one of the baskets that he had hoped to fill with quite a different catch.

Suddenly the baby began to speak in verse, and Elphin then knew that the baby was magical. Because of the young boy's beauty, he decided to name him Taliesin or 'Radiant Brow.' He carried the child home with him, on the back of his horse to his wife Ellyw, who cared for the boy like he was their own son.

And the day of Elphin's discovery of the baby poet was the eve of the festival of Beltane.

Taliesin later became a bard, winning much fame and fortune for Elphin at the court of Maelgwn.

126

BRITTANY

THE ANCIENT NAME for Brittany was Armorica, the land of the sea. In the fifth and sixth centuries, Brittany was peopled by Celtic refugees; hermits and missionaries who had sailed from Ireland, Wales and Cornwall. These settlers were Brittany's earliest heroes, escaping the invading hordes of Angles and Saxons and struggling to defend the Celtic faith. Yet for all their holiness, these pioneers had much in common with the warriors of other Celtic myths, as they battled against dragons, tyrants and sorcerers to lay the foundations of their independent nation.

THE BARZAZ BREIZ

THE BARZAZ BREIZ, or *Songs of Brittany*, is an anthology of poems, tales and ballads, written down in the nineteenth century by a Breton, Théodore Hersart de la Villemarqué. A native of Quimperlé, Villemarqué collected his material from remote villages, crossing the misty heaths dotted with ancient megaliths and swathed in an atmosphere of mystery. Published in 1838 and coinciding with Lady Charlotte Guest's translation of *The Mabinogion*, *The Barzaz Breiz* was highly praised, and led to wider recognition of Brittany's cultural heritage.

In the fifth and sixth centuries, a huge influx of Celtic settlers crossed the sea from places such as Cornwall and Wales. Among them were missionaries who spearheaded the gradual conversion of the region. Brittany's Celtic stories are set in this period of change. The old pagan ways were dying out, but the mysterious and magical elements of the early Celtic stories simply attached themselves to the new religion. The tales and poems were passed down orally through the centuries, forming the core of Breton history. Marie de France, writing in the twelfth century, referred to some of them, and Albert Legrand's anthology of saints' lives (1636) was another invaluable source. Yet it was *The Barzaz Breiz* that finally introduced Breton culture to a wider audience.

THE PLOTS

These stories give a fascinating insight into Brittany's Celtic past, from the paganism of cruel punishment to redemption by the early saints. Each tale is set against the shadowy backdrop of a nation that is struggling to come to terms with a new faith. In 'The Drowned City of Ys', King Gradlon is torn between his devotion to his beautiful but debauched daughter and the pangs of his own conscience. As the waves rise around Ys, he is forced to make a terrible decision.

In 'The Quest of Saint Efflam and King Arthur', an Irish prince comes to the aid of a famous Celtic hero, as he battles against a fearsome dragon. The violent and tragic story of 'Conomor and Triphine', meanwhile, tells of Count Conomor, the Breton Bluebeard. He has already slain five wives and now, it seems, the virtuous Triphine is about to become his next victim.

THE CHARACTERS

Gradlon The king of Cornouaille who rules Ys. He pays a terrible price to save his kingdom.

Dahut Gradlon's wicked daughter whose behaviour brings about the downfall of Ys.

Conomor A powerful count who plots to kill five of his wives.

Triphine Daughter of Varoch and the sixth wife of Conomor.

Gildas A Celtic saint, who tries to come to Triphine's assistance.

Efflam An Irish Prince, who flees from his wife and homeland.

Enora Prince Efflam's new bride.

St Guénolé One of the most notable saints of Brittany, who establishes the Abbey of Landévennec (see page 137).

THE DROWNED CITY OF YS

 NBEKNOWN TO MANY people there is an ancient song, which the Bretons sing about their lost city of Ys. 'Have you heard what the wise man said to Gradlon?' it begins. 'Never be ruled by love; never be ruled by folly; for sorrow follows pleasure. He who tastes the flesh of fish will himself be eaten up by them; he who consumes will be swallowed up in his turn; he who drinks too much wine will end up drinking water like a minnow.'

This Gradlon was a great and noble king, who lived in the fifth century after Our Lord. His kingdom was Cornouaille, in the southern part of Brittany, and his capital was the fair city of Quimper. He was a just man, much loved by his subjects, though some might say that he showed too much indulgence towards his daughter, the beautiful Dahut. With her pale skin, her wild, flowing hair, and her disdainful manner, she was always the centre of attention. Yet, for all that, she never seemed truly content amid the earthbound pleasures of her father's court. Some ascribed this to her youthful years, while others claimed that the strangeness was in her blood; that she owed it to the mother she had never known.

For many years, fanciful rumours had circulated about Gradlon's former queen. Some said that she was not human; that she was a fairy creature of the deep, who had taken on mortal form in order to woo the handsome king of Cornouaille. For a time, they had been happy and Dahut had been the product of their love. But, so the story went, Gradlon had offended his mate and she fled back to the sea, leaving him to bring up their daughter alone. None of Gradlon's subjects knew if this was true, of course, but some felt that it explained the wistful look that came into Dahut's eyes, whenever she gazed out to sea.

Gradlon's relationship with his daughter deteriorated, after he rejected his pagan ways and became a Christian. This conversion came about in an unexpected manner. One day, the king and his men were out hunting in the forest near Menez-Hom. The sport was good and, after a while, the hounds caught the scent of a boar. This led them off their usual track and took them on a merry chase through mires and thickets; through wide clearings and along dank streams. For several hours, the huntsmen galloped in pursuit, taking no note of the route they were following. At last, the horses became exhausted and Gradlon was forced to call a halt. Only then, when the huntsmen looked about them, did they realize that they were completely lost.

By now it was late afternoon, so Gradlon told his men to scout around the area, to see if they could find a pathway out of the forest before it grew dark. Within minutes, one of them returned, saying that he had come across a woodman's hut. So, together, the king and his companions rode towards the shack, hoping that the occupant would be able to give them directions.

When they reached the place, however, they found that it was not occupied by a woodman, but by a hermit named Corentin. Even though he was not a Christian, Gradlon had heard of the man, and was familiar with his reputation for holiness and good works. So he greeted the hermit warmly and asked him if he could help them find their homeward path. 'Gladly,' replied Corentin, 'but I see from the state of your horses that you have come a long way. Might I not offer you some refreshment, before you embark on your lengthy journey?'

The king readily agreed to the hermit's generous invitation, and he went to sit with his host while his men busied themselves in tending to the horses. The two men conversed for some time, and Gradlon was immediately impressed by the hermit's great knowledge and understanding. Yet some of the huntsmen were less enthusiastic. 'Are we going to dine on prayers and paternosters alone?' they whispered to each other. 'Does this monk not realize that we have been riding since dawn, without stopping to eat so much as a morsel?'

In fact, Corentin was well aware of their hunger and, rising from his place, he beckoned to two of the king's servants to follow him. Bidding them bring their largest basket and their most capacious ewer, he led them to the other side of the hut. There they found a small well, in which a tiny fish was swimming. First, Corentin took the ewer and filled it with water from the well. Then he fished out the minnow with his hands, cut it in two with his knife, and put one of the halves in the basket. The other half, he threw back into the well. Corentin then instructed the men to go and place these vessels on the cloth, where the king was to have his feast. Initially, they refused, thinking that the hermit was jesting with them. But Corentin was insistent, so eventually they obeyed. Then the servants went to the king and his fellow-huntsmen, informing them that the food provided by their host was ready. They warned, however, that it was meagre fare and would do little to satisfy their hunger.

Imagine their surprise, therefore, when they beheld the sight that awaited them. The cloth was laid with dainties of every kind. Meat, fish and fruit were there in abundance, and the ewer was full to the brim with a dark red wine. Gradlon marvelled greatly when he heard what the hermit had achieved. His wonder increased still further when the holy man took him to the well and showed him the fish that had provided their feast. The half that had been thrown back was whole again, swimming around as if nothing had happened.

When the time came to leave, Gradlon was reluctant to part without the hermit. 'Why do you remain here in solitude?' he asked Corentin. 'If you wish to spread the word of your God, then come back with me to my capital,' he implored. 'Be among men, and spread your faith throughout my kingdom; I will make you bishop of Quimper and you may make as many converts as you will.' Although the hermit was sorry to leave his woody retreat, the opportunity to do such great service for the Lord was irresistible. He agreed at once.

In this manner, Gradlon became a Christian and the ways of Quimper were changed forever. Churches, chapels and cloisters were erected, to meet the needs of the faithful. In addition, Corentin urged the king to pass new laws, curbing the excesses of the flesh and promoting virtue, charity and temperance in their stead.

Months passed, and Gradlon noticed the effect of all the changes he had made. Quimper had become a worthier, more contented place.

Only one thing marred the king's pleasure and that was the attitude of his daughter, Dahut. She grew listless and moody. Nothing seemed to satisfy her, and her pallor became more marked, as if she were wasting away into a phantom. At last, the king spoke to her about this: 'My child, what ails you? Are you sickening for something?'

'It is this terrible place, my father. You have filled it with monks and penitents. There is no joy, no laughter here anymore; only the sound of prayers and chanting.'

'Silence, my child,' he answered. 'You must not blaspheme against the servants of the Lord. The value of their work outweighs all other considerations.'

Then Dahut lowered her head and began to sob. Immediately, Gradlon's heart softened and he began to wonder if he was being too harsh on the child. 'There, little one, don't cry so. Is there nothing I could do to ease your cares? You know, you only have to ask and it shall be yours.'

Dahut's eyes lit up. There is one thing ...' she said, in her gentlest voice.

'Ask away, child,' he replied.

'The sea, father. I want the sea.' Gradlon looked puzzled, so she continued: 'I miss the sea. I cannot bear to live so far away from it. Build me a city by the sea and I will be content.'

Thus it was that the city of Ys came to be built. A site was chosen at the westernmost tip of Cornouaille, near the Pointe du Raz. From there, Dahut could gaze out across the ocean, towards the edge of the world. Gradlon instructed his workmen to spare no expense and soon the city began to take shape. Tall white towers loomed up by the water's edge, overlooking the broad, gracious avenues and spacious public squares. Indeed, the results were so splendid that Gradlon decided to join his daughter and transfer his court to the new city, leaving Corentin to administer the city of Quimper. Dahut was delighted. She planted a thousand kisses on the king's cheek and the palace rang with the sound of her laughter. Like any devoted father, Gradlon could have wished for nothing more.

The court had not been long in Ys, however, when Gradlon received a messenger from Corentin. 'Where,' the bishop enquired, 'was the house of God in this splendid new city of his?' Gradlon hung his head in shame. In his anxiousness to please his daughter, he had neglected to build a church. Immediately, he sent back word to the cleric that he would rectify his mistake.

Dahut, meanwhile, approached him with a different request. The city of Ys had been built in a hollow, she pointed out, and it was vulnerable to any flood or storm. She suggested, therefore, that his architects should waste no time in constructing a dyke, to protect the city from the waves. Gradlon listened to her patiently and promised to consider the matter. Yet he knew that his first priority was to build a church; without the House of God, his mortal soul and those of all his subjects might be imperilled.

No argument could have filled Dahut with greater rage. In an instant, she imagined how her precious city would be turned into another Quimper, suffocated by monks and preachers. She stamped off, determined to find her own way to prevent this.

The instincts of her mother offered Dahut the solution to her problem. In the dead of night, she stole out of bed and made her way down to the harbour. Climbing aboard a boat, she set off for the island of Sein. Although this was not far from Ys, the waters around the isle were treacherous and local fishermen had coined a saying, 'Qui voit Sein, voit sa fin' (He who sees Sein, meets his end). Despite this, Dahut was determined to reach the place. For she knew that on Sein there was a sisterhood of priestesses who kept to the old ways, expelling all who attempted to preach the Gospel. These women had the power to cast enchantments; to heal the sick or poison their enemies; to raise storms and cause shipwrecks. More than this, they could command the Korrigans, a dwarfish race of elves who had the strength and speed of a hundred men.

When she arrived at the island, Dahut could see no sign of the sisters. She searched along the lonely shore; she clambered over the perilous rocks, where so many sailors had met their doom; and then she headed inland, stepping fearlessly onto the winding path that led into the silent darkness of the forest. At last, she found them in a clearing, gathered in a circle around the dying embers of a fire. Bravely, she entered the ring and addressed them: 'Hear me, women of Sein. I am Dahut, mistress of Ys, and I have come to crave your assistance.'

The oldest of the women approached her. 'We know of you, Dahut, daughter of Gradlon. Your name is still uttered in those places where the old gods are worshipped. But what brings you to Sein? Few come to visit us now, persecuted as we are by those of the new faith. They have driven us out of the heaths and the fields and the villages. The darkness of the forest is all that we have left. There is no other place for us.'

Dahut sympathized with their plight, explaining that her city, too, lay under threat from the men of God. So the women agreed to help her. They conjured up the Korrigans and ordered them to construct a dyke around the city. In addition, they were to fashion a new castle, one that was both elegant and imposing, and to ensure that it towered over Gradlon's church. All these things were to be performed before the first light of day broke over Ys.

Dahut thanked the women profusely and returned to her boat. It did not take her long to travel back to Ys but, as she drew close, she was delighted to glimpse the turrets of her new castle, all white and gleaming in the moonlight. Then, as she came towards the harbour, she saw the stout sea-wall that she had been promised. It was made from massive blocks of stone, three cubits thick, and it appeared strong enough to withstand any storm. The dyke was controlled by a bronze sluice-gate, and this gate could be opened with two silver keys. Dahut found them sitting in their respective locks, as she reached the wall. Carefully she took out the keys and handed them to Gradlon for safe-keeping. He marvelled at the improvements that had been made to the city, and tried to question his daughter about them. But Dahut concealed the truth from him, saying only that she had hired her own architects.

In the months that followed, the splendour of Ys was matched by its prosperity. With the aid of the Korrigans, Dahut found new ways of enriching its citizens. She bought them finer boats, faster and stronger, so that they would not perish in the gales and tempests that were commonplace near that stretch of the coast. Then, from the depths of the ocean, she summoned up terrible monsters that preyed upon passing ships, driving them onto the rocks. Soon, the inhabitants of Ys turned from fishermen into scavengers, filling their coffers with the jewels, the spices, and other precious cargoes that were washed ashore from the ruined hulks. No one was more greedy for these treasures than Dahut herself. At night, she used to wander down to the shore and call upon the Korrigans to bring her some new toy: a piece of coral for her hair, a bauble to hang around her neck, a drowning sailor for a lover. And each of these trinkets pleased her only for a moment. Then, tiring of them, she cast them back into the foaming water.

It did not take long for the citizens of Ys to be corrupted by the ease of their newfound wealth. Gradlon's church became neglected, as the inhabitants gave themselves over to a life of luxury and fornication. This lamentable state of affairs could not continue. After a time, Corentin called for Guénolé, the head of the abbey of Landévennec, and told him to go and preach to the people of Ys about the error of their ways.

Guénolé was appalled when he witnessed at first-hand the vice that lay at the heart of the city. The church that had been built so recently was deserted. On the exterior, weeds were forcing their way through cracks in the masonry while, inside, dust lay thick on the benches and the altars. Guénolé realized that there was no point in waiting for a congregation to arrive. Instead, he stood in the street outside the building and delivered his message. With a loud voice, he urged the inhabitants to change their evil ways and repent. Otherwise, he assured them, the Lord would bring destruction down upon them all.

Guénolé's words were greeted with derision. 'Who is this beggar?' cried the crowd, mocking the poor garments of the holy man. Then they began to hurl stones at him, chasing him away from the precincts of the church and forcing him to flee beyond the city walls.

Dahut, meanwhile, ruled Ys in all but name. Gradlon bore

the crown and carried the sceptre, but he could refuse his daughter nothing, bewitched as he was by paternal love. He did not know, or wish to know, the atrocities that were committed inside her castle. Instead, he retired alone to his apartments and went early to his bed.

Moderation of this kind was alien to Dahut. Each night, her palace of the Korrigans echoed with the sounds of feasting and carousing. Each night, too, there seemed to be a different suitor at her side. For, the reputation of this pale beauty had spread far and wide. From every part of Brittany, young noblemen travelled to look on her, and fall under her spell. Dahut never disappointed them. Throughout the evening, she would nuzzle up to her companions, offering them wine from her goblet and fruit from her own hand. Then she would whisper in their ears or toss her hair, so that a waft of perfume drifted over them, making them drunk with desire for her.

For a favoured few, the princess offered more private delights. She would send an attendant, a tall man wrapped in a jet-black cloak, to instruct her chosen man. The suitor in question was given a silken mask, and ordered to wear it when entering or leaving her chamber. In this way, he was told, no scandal would be attached to her name. The attendant fetched the man at dusk, leading him through secret corridors to Dahut's room, and the lover stole away at dawn.

This procedure would be repeated for as long as it pleased the princess. Eventually, when she grew tired of her admirer, she would make a point of tying the ribbons of his mask with a special knot. Then, as her lover left the chamber, he would feel the mask tighten on his face. In a moment, the silk ribbons turned to iron, and the wires pressed in on the man's skull, crushing it like a flimsy shell. At this juncture, the retainer would carry the victim away on his horse, as far as the Pointe du Raz. There, he would lift the body from the saddle and hurl it into the sea. Local fishermen came to know the truth of this only too well. For they soon recognized the cries of tormented souls in the sound of the wind, as it howled around the cape.

Dahut herself remained immune to the charms of her many suitors. None of them made her wish for the sound of wedding bells. None of them, at least, until a stranger from a foreign land entered the walls of Ys. He came with a magnificent train of followers, bearing the princess a rich array of gifts. The knight himself was clad entirely in red, from the crest on his helmet to the spurs on his feet. Even his beard was as red as the flames of hell. And, instead of a page, he was attended by a hunchbacked dwarf, who covered his deformity with an old goatskin.

This stranger stood apart from all the other suitors. He did not rush to sit beside the princess in the feasting hall, nor would he join in her lovers' games. When she sent him the silken mask, he refused to wear it, arriving bare-faced in her chamber. Dahut feigned anger, saying that her honour would be compromised, but secretly she was intrigued by his self-control. He appeared able to resist her charms, where no other could. At length, she reached out a hand so could caress his cheek, hoping to give him some encouragement.

But the man drew back. 'What will you give me, princess?' he asked.

'Am I not gift enough for you?' she replied, surprised by his impudence.

'Will you give me what I ask you?' he retorted.

'Ask, and I may consider it,' she answered.

'Do you like me enough to give me the keys to your sea-wall?'

'Impossible,' she said. 'Gradlon wears them around his neck, day and night. He will never let you have them.'

'It is night, princess,' the man said. 'He will be asleep. Surely, it would not be difficult for you to steal the keys from him?'

Dahut hesitated, so the man continued. 'Give them to me, princess, and I will make you my bride. I will carry you off to my palace of fire, with its columns of smoke.'

At last, curiosity got the better of Dahut. Stealthily, she ushered the man out of her chamber and down the maze of passageways, which led to Gradlon's apartments. Soon, they were at the entrance to his bedchamber. Dahut peeped inside and saw that her father was fast asleep. On tip-toe, she crept into the room, towards the bed. Outside, a storm was rising, so she felt confident that her footsteps would not be heard. She stretched out a hand and eased the keys off the chain, that the king wore about his neck. Then, without looking round, she passed them back to her companion. Warm fingers tugged the keys away from her. Now Dahut turned her head, hoping to see a smile on her lover's face. But she saw no such thing, for the stranger was no longer there

LANDÉVENNEC

THE ABBEY OF Landévennec is situated on the Crozon peninsula, some twenty-five miles north-west of Quimper. It provides us with our most tangible link to the legend of Ys, since two of the main characters – St Guénolé and Gradlon – are thought to have been buried there. In addition, the foundation of the abbey itself is traditionally ascribed to Guénolé, although no traces of his fifth-century settlement can be found. Early accounts of the saint's life describe him as the son of a Welsh prince named Fracan, who migrated to an island near the Breton coast, defended it from pirates, and used the spoils to build a monastery there. Although there is no apparent historical basis for any of these details, it is certain, nonetheless, that Landévennec rapidly became an important religious centre and that it maintained strong contacts with other Celtic lands. The influence of Irish monasticism was more pronounced at Landévennec than at any other Breton foundation, and this may account for the persistent legend that Guénolé wished to join St Patrick in Ireland.

In addition, the cult of the saint spread across the Channel to Cornwall. In fact, five Cornish churches are dedicated to him under his anglicized form, St Winwaloe.

The king woke from his sleep with a start. Someone was calling out to him. 'Flee for your life, Gradlon. The sluice-gates are open and Ys is being flooded. Soon, the whole city will be under the sea.' The king opened his eyes and saw the figure of Guénolé, pulling at his shoulder. He also heard the crashing of the waves, as they pummelled the walls of his castle.

There was no time to lose. Gradlon leaped out of bed and ran for the door. As always, his first thought was for his daughter. He must rescue her at all cost. Leaving his room, he headed immediately for her apartments, hoping against hope that he could reach her in time. In fact, he did not have to go very far to find her. For Dahut was standing in a corridor outside his chamber, frozen in a state of complete bewilderment. Gradlon grabbed her by the hand and led her down the stairs. In the courtyard, Guénolé was waiting for him with his horse. In an instant, he mounted the beast and pulled his daughter up behind him. Then, accompanied by the monk, he quickly rode towards the city gate.

Guénolé's horse made swift progress, but Gradlon's charger lagged behind. It seemed to him that the animal moved slowly, as if it were bearing the weight of three men on its back. Guénolé turned round in his saddle and recognized the problem immediately. 'Cast off the demon that is riding behind you,' he called out.

But the king ignored his advice, digging his heels into the horse's side. To no avail, for the waters continued to rise round the animal's legs.

'Cast off the demon, Gradlon, or you will be lost,' Guénolé called once more.

'What are you saying, monk? This is my daughter, not a demon.'

But the holy man shook his head. 'She is the cause of all your woes. It is she who has given the keys of the sea-wall to the devil and brought ruin upon your city of Ys. Cast her off this instant, I say, or you will perish with her.'

Gradlon still hesitated, so then Guénolé reached across him with his staff and struck Dahut on the shoulder. Straight away, the princess lost her grip and, with a cry, she fell backwards into the torrent. Immediately, the waters swallowed her up and she was seen no more. At this very moment, the storm began to subside, and Gradlon and Guénolé were able to ride away to safe ground. When they finally reached dry land, Gradlon rested his horse and tried to come to terms with the sudden tragedy that had cost the life of his beloved daughter. A church named Poul-Dahut was later erected on this spot.

After some time when they had both recovered their strength, Guénolé decided to lead the king back to the abbey of Landévennec. They soon lost sight of the sea, but a terrible mist followed in their wake, pursuing them like some relentless ghost. And, in this half-blind state, every gull's cry caused Gradlon to start in his saddle, as he recalled the last screams of the daughter that he had left behind.

Gradlon remained at Guénolé's abbey for several months. But Landévennec, like Ys, was built close to the water's edge, so the king was never truly able to relax. At night, the sound of the waves lapping against the shore drove him to distraction, keeping him from his slumbers. Instead, he used to sit at the window of his cell and gaze sadly out across the moonlit waters. Sometimes, he thought he could hear his daughter calling out to him. But now her voice was no longer anguished, as it had been on the night of the flood, but sweet; so sweet, in fact, that he was filled with a truly powerful longing to leap into the water and seek her out, wherever she was.

Gradlon was not alone in hearing such a wonderful voice. After Dahut's disappearance, many fishermen reported seeing a mermaid in the waters near the Pointe du Raz. Her form was beautiful, they said, and her long hair floated gently on the surface of the water. But it was her songs that they all remembered the best. For because she sang so plaintively, many of those who heard her voice swam out in search of her. And, if they actually found her, they never returned to the shore again.

After a time, Gradlon could no longer bear to be near the sea, and he fled away from the abbey. Guénolé was very concerned at his disappearance and anxiously set out to look for him. Following a long search, he found him in the forest of Kranou, where he was lying on his deathbed. With faltering words, the king told Guénolé that he had been living as a hermit, with a solitary druid as his only companion. 'Do not be harsh on the old man,' he urged Guénolé, 'for he has lived for three ages and has suffered far more than I have. It is true that I have lost my daughter and my chief city, but this man has lost his gods. He mourns a dead religion. What sorrow can ever compare with that loss?'

These were Gradlon's last words before he died. The druid informed Guénolé that his final wish had been for a church to be erected on the site. In time, this was accomplished, and the new building was given the name of Rumengol. Guénolé, meanwhile, invited the druid to return with him and live out his remaining days in the shelter of Landévennec.

However, the druid refused, saying to Guénolé: 'For me, the woodland paths are better. Who knows, perhaps they may lead to the same great centre of existence that you also seek.' With that, he turned away from the monk and walked back into his beloved forest. Guénolé then took Gradlon's body back to his abbey, where it was buried with great reverence and ceremony.

And what became of the city of Ys itself? Some people say that it lives on under the sea, invisible to the eyes of the people living on the land. Others claim that the city was submerged just as Mass was being said in Gradlon's church. The belief is that it is being said still, but the priest cannot complete the service, because no one is there in the church to chant all the necessary responses. When a living person finally enters that church and helps the priest to finish the Mass, so the story goes, Ys will rise up again from the depths of the sea and will prove itself to be the fairest city in all of France.

CARNAC STONES

THE EXTENSIVE prehistoric remains at Carnac form one of the wonders of ancient Europe. The five thousand menhirs in the area are dominated by the three great alignments of Ménec, Kermario and Kerlescan. These date back to Neolithic times, but their precise date and function are uncertain. The fact that Kermario means 'House of the Dead' points to an old belief that the stones were associated with funerary rites, while modern archaeologists tend to hold the view that they served some astronomical purpose. Their task has been hampered by the 'restoration' that took place at the end of the nineteenth century, when many stones were re-erected and the original orientation of the lines was lost.

The stones of Carnac predate the earliest Celtic settlers, but they figure strongly in many early legends and they were seen by later generations of Frenchmen as a Celtic creation. The most colourful of the myths surrounds St Cornély, the patron saint of Carnac. Locals identified him with Pope Cornelius, whose brief tenure of the post (251–3) ended with his expulsion from Rome. In reality, the pope was banished to Civitavecchia but, in the Breton version of events, he fled to Carnac, pursued by the Roman army. When he reached the sea, he turned around and prayed for salvation. At this, his persecutors froze in their tracks, becoming the petrified host of Carnac. The papal link probably came about only because of the similarity of the two names. St Cornély himself is regarded locally as a protector of horned animals ('corne' meaning 'horn'), but he may be a Christianized form of a heathen deity, because a pagan bull cult once flourished at Carnac.

In the early nineteenth century, when the Celtic revival in France was in full flow, several writers made extravagant claims about Carnac. They described it as a huge druid temple, adding that the gaps between the alignments had once been filled with housing for the druids and for the pilgrims who came to visit the site. On a more lurid note, they added that the flat surfaces of the dolmens were used as sacrificial altars.

The stories about the druids are largely fanciful, but the early Bretons did attach great importance to the megaliths in their region. In many instances, the stones inspired pagan superstitions, and these survived long into the Christian era. In view of their phallic shape, it is hardly surprising that most of these superstitions should have related to fertility. At Kerloas in Finestère, for example, there stands one of the tallest menhirs in Brittany. For centuries, newly-weds used to go there by night and dance naked around the stone, in the hope that this would bring them sons. The practice still existed in the nineteenth century although, by this time, the participants were clothed.

Missionaries adapted the stones to their own uses by carving Christian symbols on them. Some of these markings were very elaborate; at St Uzec, for example, they included images of the Virgin and the Instruments of the Passion. Elsewhere, the heathen associations of the stones were simply overlaid with Christian legends. Thus, there is a story that the menhir of Champ-Dolent was really a boulder, which St Samson threw at the devil, while the eight small stones at Lanrivoaré are supposed to be loaves petrified by St Hervé, to punish a baker who had refused him alms.

THE QUEST OF SAINT EFFLAM AND KING ARTHUR

 ANY LONG YEARS went by when war raged between the peoples of Ireland and Albion. At last, after two whole generations had passed, both sides were tired of fighting and decided to make peace. This was their plan: a son had recently been born to the Irish king and a daughter to the king of Albion. It was agreed that, when they reached a suitable age, they would be married, and a bond of peace would be forged between the two peoples. And the names of these children were Efflam and Enora.

Prince Efflam grew up into a strong and handsome lad, courageous at heart and noble in spirit. He was also well-educated and pious, for his father had entrusted his upbringing to the care of a community of monks. They had inspired in the boy a sincere love for the words of Our Lord and a great willingness to do anything in His service. As a result, Efflam took little interest in the affairs of court and had no great desire to follow his father as king. Nor did he feel any attraction towards marriage, for the monks had taught him to prize chastity above all else. So, as the date of his wedding approached, he resolved to flee across the water to Armorica. There, he intended to live out his days as a hermit, meditating on the sufferings of Our Lord. To this end, he instructed some of his companions to make ready a boat, so that he might secretly flee from Ireland.

But the king came to learn of his plan, and he summoned Efflam into his presence. Patiently, he explained to his son how the peace and wellbeing of two peoples was dependent upon the marriage. Without it, there would be many widowed mothers and many fatherless children in the land. So, with a heavy heart, the prince changed his mind and agreed to wed Enora.

The chief nobles from both kingdoms assembled at the Irish court, and the wedding was celebrated with great feasting. Everyone praised the beauty of Enora. She, for her part, was immediately taken with Efflam's good looks and thought herself exceedingly fortunate in the match that had been arranged for her.

Eventually, it grew late, and everyone retired to bed. At last, the couple were alone in the bridal chamber. Now Efflam began to speak earnestly to his new wife, explaining the promises that he had made to the monks and how he had sworn to spend his life in solitude and chastity. He even told her of his plan to flee across the sea to Armorica. Enora wept bitterly.

At once, Efflam regretted having opened his heart to her. With soothing words, he calmed her fears and wiped away her tears. 'Let us live as brother and sister for the moment,' he suggested, 'until we can find a solution that suits us both. We can talk further in the morning.' This comforted her somewhat, so she agreed and lay down to sleep.

When he was sure that Enora was fast asleep, Efflam crept out of bed and stole out of the chamber. Swiftly, he made his way down to the harbour, where his companions were waiting with a boat. Under cover of darkness, they set sail and, by morning, they were long gone.

Now, at that time, the Breton countryside was a wild place, ravaged by many foul beasts and monsters. The most terrible of these creatures was a fearsome dragon that was laying waste to the thickly-wooded district around Lannion. To rid themselves of this monster, the Bretons had enlisted the aid of a great champion from across the water. This was Arthur of Britain. He had recently slain the giant of Mont-St-Michel and now he had travelled west, to come to the aid of the citizens of Lannion. With skill and courage, he had tracked the beast through perilous, tangled forests, until he came upon its lair. This was a huge cavern, nine cubits deep, situated by the sandy shoreline of the Lieue de Grève. Close by, there was a massive boulder known as the Hyrglas or the Long Green Rock. Arthur spotted the clawprints of the beast, showing how it had left its cave and made its way along the beach. Accordingly, he sent out some of his knights to patrol the surrounding area, while he remained with the rest at the entrance to the cave, awaiting the creature's return. But this was a subtle beast. To avoid being trapped in its lair, it had developed the habit of entering it backwards, so that potential enemies would think it was absent. Now, at this very moment, it was lurking in the depths of the cavern, waiting to pounce on its new victims.

As Arthur sat by the shore, unaware of this, he noticed a boat on the horizon. In due course, this came to ground by the Hyrglas and a group of young men descended. At their head was a handsome youth, tall and fair, with the manners of a prince. The youth greeted him cordially, saying: 'I am Efflam, only son of the king of Ireland. Pray, good sir, could you tell me where I am?'

With this, Arthur embraced the young man joyfully, explaining that they were cousins. Then he listened while Efflam told him everything; how he was fleeing from an unwelcome marriage and how he proposed to live a life of quiet contemplation in his new home.

Arthur was amused by this final comment. 'My friend, you have chosen a curious spot for such a life as this. Do you not know that this wild coast is the haunt of dangerous demons? Even now, I am here to confront a monster so dreadful that the very sight of him strikes most men dead. Certainly, it is not the place for an unarmed man, who is little used to fighting.'

'The servants of God fear nothing,' Efflam replied, 'for they know that they are safe in the protection of the good and mighty Saviour.'

'If that is so,' said Arthur, 'then I pray you, cousin, wait and be a witness to my combat. For it cannot be long now before the dragon returns to its lair.'

'He is there, as we speak,' said Efflam. 'I saw him as my boat approached the shore. He came a little way out of the cave, when you were looking out to sea, and then retreated inside it again.'

On hearing this, Arthur went and made ready for battle. He put on his coat of mail and his golden helmet, with its dragon-like emblem. About his shoulders, he buckled his shield Priwén, on which there was a likeness of the Blessed Mary. Then he took up his fine sword Calibrus, forged at the nearby island of Aval, and girded it about his waist. Finally, in his right hand, he grasped the lance named Ron, which was hard, broad and fit for slaughter. Armed with these, Arthur approached the cavern, giving many a loud shout to lure out his foe.

Now the dragon came out of its lair, vile and steaming. It had a single red eye in the middle of its forehead and its body was covered in heavy, green scales. It had the form of a fully-grown bull, but its tail was twisted into a spiral, like an iron screw, and there were needle-sharp horns at every joint, to deter any attacker from coming too close.

Arthur advanced towards the beast, and laid into it with his sword and lance. The battle was long and fierce, and not without casualties. At one point, Arthur's horse was gored by one of the horns and it fell to the ground, with blood pouring from its nostrils. But Arthur disentangled himself from his fallen mount and continued to fight on foot. The battle lasted for three days and three nights without a break. At the end of this time, the beast retired into its den and Arthur collapsed on the sand, exhausted and thirsty. But there was no fresh water to be had, so Efflam fell to his knees and began praying earnestly. At length, he rose up and, after making the sign of the cross, he struck the Hyrglas three times with his staff. At once, a fountain opened up in the face of the rock and pure, clean water gushed out onto the beach. Arthur drank gratefully from this miraculous spring and, as he did so, the waters healed his wounds. From this time on, the place was known as Toul-Efflam, and pilgrims began to travel there, to seek a cure for their infirmities.

'And now, good cousin,' said the prince, 'I pray you, leave this affair in my hands. We shall see what the power of prayer can do.' Whereupon, he and his companions fasted and humbled themselves before the Lord. All night long they prayed until, shortly after the first light of morning, Efflam got to his feet and walked to the mouth of the cavern. With a commanding voice, he ordered the beast to come out of its hiding place. And the beast obeyed, rolling its terrible eye and hissing with the sound of a thousand snakes. Like a thing enchanted, it followed Efflam back to the Hyrglas, clambered to its summit, and then threw itself into the sea with a clamorous roar. There, it sank miserably beneath the waves, leaving a swirl of blood-soaked bubbles in its wake.

The two cousins celebrated this triumph, and Arthur invited the Irishman to return with him to his court. Efflam would not be deflected from his religious purpose, however, so Arthur made his farewells and left to seek out new adventures.

The prince then explored his new home and, after a while, they found an abandoned, ramshackle hut. Efflam decided to take this for himself and he ordered his men to build similar shelters. In this isolated land, they would devote themselves fully to the service of God.

In Ireland, Efflam's disappearance had been greeted with dismay. No one felt this sorrow more keenly than Enora. Her tears flowed day and night, and none of her waiting-women could console her. At length, she knew that life without her husband would not be worth living and she decided to follow him, no matter how perilous the journey. So, she set out to sea in a frail craft, made out of wicker-work and animal hides.

The crossing lasted three days, before her boat found its way into the mouth of the river Léguer. There, it became tangled up with some fishing nets belonging to a local lord. Enora was released from these by a humble fisherman, who was astonished to find such a beauteous prize caught amid the meshes. The princess thanked him profusely and asked him if he had heard any news of a young Irish prince, who had come to Armorica to live as a recluse.

BELTANE

An intricately decorated fragment of goldwork found at a shrine: the figure may represent the god Belenus.

THE BEST-KNOWN of the Celtic seasonal festivals, Beltane was celebrated on 1 May and coincided with the start of summer and the open pasturing of livestock. The name derives from 'Bel-tinne' ('the fires of Bel'), suggesting that the festival was originally devoted to the god Belenus. The latter was a Gaulish sun god, worshipped under different guises in many parts of the Celtic world. The Romans likened him to Apollo; classical authors linked him with shrines in Provençe, Burgundy and northern Italy. His memory also survives in a host of proper names, among them the British king Cymbeline (or Cunobelin, 'hound of Belenus') and Billingsgate, London. Beltane was a fire festival, marked with bonfires on hilltops and other sacred places. In Ireland, it was customary to drive cattle between two druidic fires, to gain protection from disease. Beltane was the most enduring of the Celtic festivals. In parts of Scotland it survived into the eighteenth century, giving its name to one of the old quarter-days. Expatriate Scots established Beltane Fairs as far afield as Canada and South Africa. The evening preceding the festival was a magical time, when witches and spirits roamed abroad. This is now known as Walpurgis Night, after St Walpurga.

Now, word of the dragon's defeat by Efflam and Arthur had spread far and wide, so the fisherman was able to give her a full account of the adventure. He also showed her the route to the prince's retreat.

Enora set off, having made the man promise that he would tell no one of her arrival. In spite of this, the fisherman felt that it was his duty to inform his master. He did this immediately, emphasizing the great beauty of the young woman. This intrigued the nobleman and he was filled with a great desire to see her. A little while later, he saw Enora walking in the distance. Straight away, he spurred on his horse, thinking to overtake her. But, even though the woman was only walking on foot, he could not catch up with her, no matter how swiftly he rode.

It was only when Enora arrived at the hut that the young nobleman was able to catch up with her. Descending from his horse, he went over to touch her on the shoulder. As he did so, however, a stiffness seized his arm and he found that it was paralysed. Falling over in alarm, he tried to steady himself by resting his other hand against the wall of the refuge. But this hand became stuck to the side of the hut and, no matter how hard he tugged, the man could not budge it.

When she saw this, Enora cried out in horror. Her cries alerted Efflam and he rushed outside to see what was happening. Swiftly, he laid his hands on the young nobleman, who was soon cured of his ills. The latter apologized profusely to Enora for having frightened her, and he rewarded Efflam by giving him the land on which he and his companions were living.

Shortly afterwards the nobleman departed, and Efflam and Enora were left alone to talk. The prince was happy to see his bride again and was relieved that she had suffered no harm on her travels, but he felt obliged to explain to her that nothing had changed between them. His desire to lead a celibate and solitary life was as strong as ever. Eventually Enora accepted this, asking only that she might be allowed to live a similar existence, not far away from him. This was readily agreed.

In this way, they spent the rest of their married lives, apart and yet in close proximity. From time to time, Enora visited the prince, although she never again spoke to him face to face. Instead, she would address him from behind a door or through her veil. Henceforward, spiritual matters were their sole topic of conversation. Over many years, reports of their holiness spread abroad and pilgrims regularly came to visit them, hoping to gain inspiration from their example.

At last, it happened that a peasant woman came to see Enora, intending to ask her to pray for a sick child. She called out her name, but there was no reply. Then, looking through an opening in the wall of the hut, she saw that Enora was lying dead on the floor. Behind her, there was a shimmering radiance and the figure of a young boy, all dressed in white. The woman rushed out to tell Efflam but, when she reached his refuge, she found him laid out in a similar fashion.

Efflam was buried on the site of the hut, his only home in Brittany. A chapel was built above his grave and this soon became a place of pilgrimage. In time, however, worshippers forgot the precise location of his tomb until a woman, whose job it was to sweep out the chapel, noticed three dark red spots on one of the paving stones. Thinking that they looked like blood, she scrubbed the floor until the spots had gone. The next day, however, they reappeared in precisely the same location. This pattern was repeated for a week, until the woman informed the bishop of Tréguier. He gave orders for the stone to be lifted and, when the workmen delved further, they came upon the bones of the holy man. These were reburied in a prominent part of the church, and Efflam's name has been revered in Brittany from that day to this.

CONOMOR AND TRIPHINE

N THE SIXTH CENTURY after Our Lord, there was in Brittany an ambitious count named Conomor. He lived in a castle in the forest of Carnot, not far from Quimperlé, but his power stretched far beyond this modest domain. Early in his career, he won new lands and honours through force of arms, for no one would deny that he was a brave and gifted warrior. As his ambitions grew, however, he realized that he could achieve much more by other, less hazardous means. Gradually, therefore, he exchanged his sword and buckler for the softer weapons of marriage and diplomacy. A few well-placed words of intrigue, he found, earned him more than a hundred spear thrusts; and a carefully chosen bride made him richer than a hundred sword blows.

Conomor's first wife was a wealthy widow with extensive lands. At first, it appeared that the count was kind and considerate to his new bride, attentive to her needs and genuinely interested in looking after this lady and her infant son. But, when the boy disappeared and his mother died suddenly from an unexplained sickness, dark rumours began to circulate in the area. The whispers grew more fierce when Conomor's next wife also met a premature end. The woman was a young heiress, barely twenty years of age, when she died in childbirth. Nor did her newborn baby boy survive her.

In public, Conomor put on a convincing show of grief but, privately, he consoled himself with the knowledge that these tragedies had helped swell his coffers. Soon he took a third wife. But this third marriage proved equally short-lived, as did the next. Suspicion mounted among his people, but no one dared to challenge the count directly. For nothing could be proved and, with each wedding, he grew richer and more powerful. Besides, no one had guessed the real reason for his actions.

This sprang from an incident that had occurred shortly before his first wedding. A few days before the event, the count had spoken with an old crone, who was known to have the gift of foresight. She warned him that, if he married, he would die by the hand of his own son. Conomor took the prophecy seriously. He had a hireling cut the throat of the widow's boy and he killed his second wife himself, as she lay in bed nursing his newborn child.

Then, as he grew more callous, he realized that even atrocities such as these might not be enough to protect him in the future. What if some serving-woman were to spirit away his infant son? What if his wife ran away when she was with child? The risk was too great, he decided.

Henceforth, any future wife of his would die as soon as it was known that she was pregnant.

It came about, in due course, that five of Conomor's wives had died and he began to cast his eyes around for a sixth. Then his gaze fell on Triphine, the daughter of Varoch, the Count of the Vannetais. She was a graceful girl, admired as much for her virtue as for her beauty, and many noble suitors had tried in vain to court her. It need hardly be said that Conomor's proposal was greeted with dismay by both Triphine and her father. At first, Varoch refused, explaining to Conomor's messengers, as discreetly as he knew how, that his daughter was too young to commit herself to marriage. But the envoys were not to be deterred so easily. One of them picked up a handful of straw and called for a lighted taper. 'Do not answer too hastily, old man,' he warned, 'for if Triphine does not become our master's bride, his displeasure will be great indeed. And his anger will pass over your country like a burning brand, razing your cornfields to stubble.' And with this, he lit the bundle of straw and threw it high into the air, so that the burning fragments flew in every direction.

Varoch was alarmed at this blatant threat of war, so he summoned his spiritual counsellor to ask him for guidance. This adviser was a hermit, the future St Gildas. He was originally from Scotland, and had trained in Wales at the school of St Illtyd. Once Conomor learned that this holy man was to mediate in the affair, he went to see him. With vigorous pleas, he protested that he was innocent of the terrible crimes that had been ascribed to him and that he was a true and loyal servant of God.

Gildas believed none of this, but he had no wish to see his adopted homeland ravaged by war.

CALVARIES

THE MOST distinctive feature of Breton churches is the parish close. This consists of three main elements: a triumphal arch, a calvary and an ossuary or charnel house. Visually, the calvary is the most impressive part of the scheme. In essence, it is a large-scale sculpture group, in which episodes from the Nativity and the Passion of Christ are displayed around a Crucifixion scene. Calvaries were sometimes employed as open-air pulpits and they often included shrines, dedicated to local Breton saints. The Biblical scenes might also include figures from Breton folklore, such as Katell Gollet (Catherine the Damned). She was a beautiful but unrepentant sinner, who stole communion wafers for the devil and, as a consequence, suffered the tortures of hell.

If the calvary is the most eye-catching part of the parish close, then the charnel house is the most central. The cult of the dead is an indispensable part of Breton culture, and the churchyard has always been the heart of the community. Whenever it was full, graves were dug up and the bones were removed to the ossuary. Sometimes, the chef (skull) was placed in a marked box, so that relatives could continue to honour it. On rare occasions, these chefs were displayed on shelves inside the church.

He also felt confident that the Lord would protect the innocent girl. So he took Triphine aside and spoke to her: 'My daughter,' he said, 'God has given you a great opportunity to make proof of your love and obedience. By becoming the wife of this Conomor, you may gain influence over him, and make him a blessing rather than a curse to the land of the black corn. In addition, you will save your own people from the horrors of war, with all its attendant sorrows and killing. Furthermore, by surrendering yourself in this way, you will be offering up a sacrifice to God, which will be as sweet incense in His nostrils.'

'Alas,' cried Triphine, 'then God is demanding the sacrifice of all my joy and happiness. How I wish now that I had been born a beggar. At least, then, I could have married the beggar of my choosing, and would never have fallen prey to the wickedness of Conomor. For, if I must give myself to this monster, then you may as well read the last offices for me today. For surely I will perish, as all his other wives have before me.'

Then Gildas reassured the maid. 'I give you my word,' he said, 'that I will bring you back to your father safe and sound.' And, as a token of his promise, he gave her a silver ring. 'Wear this always,' he advised her, 'and it will protect you from harm. For, if your husband should ever harbour any malice towards you, the ring will turn as black as a crow's wing.'

Once Gildas had given his blessing to the match, Varoch consented to the marriage. Arrangements were made and the ceremony took place soon after, amid a great show of pomp and rejoicing. The festivities lasted for a full seven days and, after this, Conomor carried his new bride back to his castle in the forest of Carnot.

The early weeks of their marriage were pleasant enough. Conomor was as courteous and attentive as any new husband might be. Triphine felt calmed by the happy atmosphere, and she wondered if her fears had been misplaced. She began to doubt the rumours; perhaps, she thought, all the tales about him are as false as he claims.

Then, some three months after the wedding, duty drew the count away from his castle. He was obliged to meet with other Breton lords at Rennes — a journey that was long and perilous.

Triphine was perfectly content in her husband's absence. She busied herself with all the wifely duties that the running of a household required; she spent long hours at needlework with her maidens, and she prayed devoutly at the chapel, where all of Conomor's previous wives were buried. To her surprise, she found that she did not miss the familiar pleasures of her father's court as much as she had expected. It was only when she realized that she was with child, that she longed to speak with Varoch and share her happiness with him. 'No matter,' she thought, 'it will not be long before he can see the infant for himself.'

At last, Conomor returned from his travels. He had missed his young wife, during their enforced separation, and was looking forward to being reunited with her.

But, as he entered her chamber, his eye was caught by the dainty little garments and baby caps that Triphine and her maidens were knitting. He found it hard to conceal the mixture of anger, sorrow and fear that consumed him. Instead, he tried to show no emotion and maintained a stony silence while an overjoyed Triphine gave him her happy news. Then he found some pretext to leave the chamber as soon as possible.

Triphine was surprised at this curious reaction, but did not regard it as greatly significant. 'Perhaps,' she thought, 'the talks at Rennes did not go well and he is weighed down with political cares.' In any event, she assumed that he would be in much better spirits after he had rested well from his journey.

A little while later, however, the lady happened to glance down at her hand. To her horror, she noticed that Gildas's ring had turned as black as night. Now she knew that her life was in imminent danger, and her first thought was to flee. But how could she leave the castle without being seen by Conomor or his soldiers? No solution came to mind. So, until she had devised a plan, she decided to hide. Where was the best place? Her first instinct was to go to the chapel for there, at least, she could pray to God for inspiration. But she knew that Conomor would look there, since her piety was well known to all. Then it occurred to her that the vault beneath the chapel would make a good place of concealment. The count's five wives were buried there and, whether out of guilt or she knew not what, he never visited that gloomy spot.

So Triphine ran to the chapel and crept down the stairs and into the darkened vault. By the flickering light of her candle, she could see that it was a large, cavernous chamber, containing nothing but six stone coffins. Five of them were covered over with heavy slabs, but the sixth coffin was empty. The sight of this filled Triphine with terror and she sank down to her knees, weeping and bewailing her fate.

When she had been kneeling for a few minutes, praying for God's assistance, she heard a grating sound. Opening her eyes, she looked over her shoulder, to see if anyone was coming down the steps. But the noise came from a closer quarter. Turning round again, Triphine realized that the coffin-slabs were moving and an eerie light was issuing from the five tombs. She stayed rooted to the spot, completely unable to move. Gradually, the ghosts of Conomor's wives rose up from their graves and faced her.

'Beware,' they cried, 'Conomor is coming to kill you, as he has killed us all. The empty coffin is for you. You have placed yourself in danger by telling him of your unborn child. The thing he fears above all else is the birth of a male child. For, it has been prophesied that he will die by the hands of his own son.'

Triphine was quivering with fear but, somehow, she found the courage to address the phantoms. 'What must I do, then? I am trapped.'

'You must return to your father,' they chorused.

'But how? There is a hound at the castle gate. I will never get past without rousing it.'

'Give the beast this poison,' said Conomor's first wife. 'It is the very same liquor that my husband gave to me, after he had cruelly murdered my young son.'

'And how can I descend from the outer wall?' continued Triphine. 'If I jump down from it, I will surely break my neck.'

'Use this rope,' said the second wife. 'It is the cord with which he strangled me.'

'Then how may I come to the road? For the forest of Carnot is thick and tangled. Without a light, I will never find my way through it.'

'Use this flame,' said the third wife. 'For it is the fire that Conomor lit around me.'

'And how will I manage on the long road back to my father?' enquired Triphine.

'Take this staff,' replied the fourth wife. 'It is the same cudgel that my husband used, when he beat me to death.'

'And what happens when my legs are too tired to walk any further?' asked Triphine in an anxious

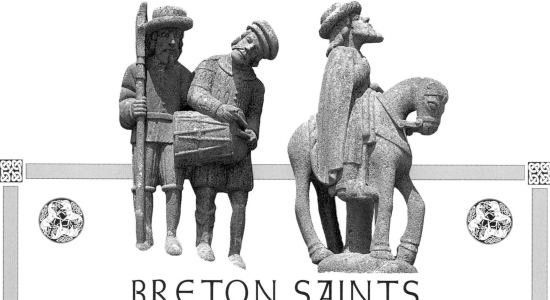

BRETON SAINTS

B<small>RITTANY HAS</small> hundreds of local saints, of which only a tiny fraction are officially recognized at Rome. Many came from other Celtic areas – Wales, Cornwall, Ireland – during the migrations of the fifth and sixth centuries. The most important figures are the seven Founding Saints (St Malo, St Brieuc, St Pol Aurélien, St Samson, St Tugdual, St Corentin and St Patern), since these are linked with the seven original bishoprics. Until the sixteenth century, every Breton was expected to make a pilgrimage, or Tro Breiz (Tour of Brittany), to visit each of their shrines. In addition, there are a host of other figures, linked to the foundation of specific monasteries or towns. The various traditions associated with their lives were collected in the seventeenth century by a monk named Albert Legrand. The historical accuracy of his book is highly debatable, but it is still a fascinating repository of Breton culture, in which Celtic and Arthurian legends are woven together with early Christian lore.

voice. 'My husband's men will surely catch up with me then.'

'When you need it, you will find a white horse,' said the fifth wife. 'Conomor tied me to it and dragged me along the ground. Now it will find a fitter purpose.'

Triphine thanked the ladies for their gifts and hurried to make her escape. At first, all went well. She poisoned the guard-dog, clambered down the castle wall and ran to the edge of the forest, where a horse awaited her. Soon she was riding along a wooded path, praying that she might return safely to her father.

It was not long, however, before Conomor realized what had happened and resolved to track her down. Swiftly summoning his finest warriors and his hunting dogs, he set off in pursuit. Triphine, meanwhile, was encountering problems. Her route led her to a rocky, mountainous pathway, where she could no longer ride. So she continued on foot, using her staff to speed her on her way. But the path kept growing narrower and narrower, until at last it petered out altogether. Triphine pressed on through the tangled thickets, but eventually she found her way blocked by the swollen waters of the river Blavet and she was not able to proceed any further. Weeping from exhaustion, she sat down by a bush to rest for a while. At this moment, she spied her father's favourite falcon circling above her in the sky. Softly, she whistled for it, and the bird came down and settled gently on her arm. Now Triphine took off her blackened ring and slipped it onto one of the creature's talons. In this way, she hoped that she might be able to warn her father that she was in danger.

This danger approached all too speedily. For, no sooner had the bird flown away, than the sound of thundering hooves became apparent. Triphine tried to struggle to her feet, but tiredness prevented her. She could only watch as her husband rode out of a thicket and came towards her. A smile of relief spread across his face. Slowly, he dismounted and walked up to her. Then, sliding his sword out of its scabbard, he struck off her head. After this, he calmly climbed back on his horse and galloped away, leaving Triphine's body lying in a clump of brambles.

It was not long before the falcon returned to Varoch's court, bearing its ominous gift. Fearing the worst, the count immediately summoned Gildas into his presence. 'You swore to my daughter that she would return to me safe and sound,' chided the old man. 'Yet is this not the ring that you gave her?' Gildas admitted that it was and after seeing the colour of the ring he promised to look into the matter straightaway. Then, using Varoch's falcon as his guide, he set out towards Conomor's castle.

The bird led Gildas straight to the bush, where Triphine was lying. With a heavy heart, the holy man knelt down beside the body

and started to pray in silence. After he had done this for some time, he uttered the following words: 'In the name of Our Lord Jesus Christ, Triphine, I command you to rise up and walk.' With this, the body began to stir and move. Soon, Triphine had revived completely. The lady's pale arms reached out in front of her and grasped her severed head, attaching it once more onto her shoulders. In a moment she was fully recovered and was as lively and beautiful as she had been on the day of her marriage to Conomor.

Joyfully, Gildas returned the girl to Varoch. 'My lord,' he said, 'I have kept my promise. Here is your daughter, safely returned to her father's house.'

Triphine suffered no ill effects from her terrible ordeal and, in due course, she gave birth to a son. After this, she was wed again, but this time she became a bride of Christ. For the remainder of her earthly life, she served as an abbess at a convent near Vannes. When she died, she was buried on the site of the bush, where Conomor had murdered her, and this place was soon revered by all as a holy shrine.

In the meantime, Gildas was determined to bring the heartless Conomor to justice. He summoned a meeting of all the holy men of Brittany, prelates both high and low, to be held on the sacred hill of Menez-Bré. This was one of the wildest and most desolate spots in the whole of the region. Even Gildas felt an eerie chill, as he climbed up toward the hill's summit. For was this not the home of Gwenc'hlan, that fearsome warrior-bard, who had been blinded and tortured by a Christian lord? And had not Gwenc'hlan sworn vengeance upon them all, as he languished in his airless dungeon?

This train of thought was suddenly interrupted, as another blind man came slowly walking into view. It was Hervé, the holiest of them all, who had been blind since birth. As usual, he was clad in his shabby hermit's skins.

'Have we been kept waiting for this wretched fellow?' said a vain bishop, dressed in all his finery. But the words were no sooner out of his mouth than he regretted saying them, for he felt his eyes grow dim and then fail completely. When informed of this tragedy, Hervé began to beat his staff against the side of the hill and suddenly, a spray of healing water spurted straight out of the soil. A servant helped the hapless bishop approach the spring and dampen his eyes with this precious water. Miraculously, his sight soon returned.

Now that the assembly was complete, judgment was passed on Conomor. Both his life and his lands were deemed to be forfeited. This sentence was eventually carried out in a most wondrous manner by Triphine's son, Tremeur. While he was still a small child, he went to his father's castle and threw a handful of earth against the outer wall. Immediately, the whole place collapsed, killing the count outright and all those people who had chosen to follow in his service.

BIBLIOGRAPHY

Berresford Ellis, P
Dictionary of Celtic Mythology, Constable, 1992

Burl, Aubrey
Megalithic Brittany, Thames & Hudson, 1985

Campbell, J J
Legends of Ireland, Batsford, 1955

Chadwick, Nora
The Celts, Pelican, 1970

Cross, T P & Slover, C
Ancient Irish Tales, George G Harrap, 1936

Dillon, Myles
Early Irish Literature,
Cambridge University Press, 1948

Eluère, Christiane
The Celts, First Masters of Europe,
Thames & Hudson, 1993

Faraday, Winifred
The Cattle Raid of Cualnge, David Nutt, 1904

Finlay, Ian
Celtic Art, Faber, 1973

Gantz, Jeffrey
The Mabinogion (trans.), Penguin, 1981
Early Irish Myths and Sagas (trans.), Penguin, 1981

Gostling, Frances M
The Bretons At Home, Methuen, 1909

Green, Miranda
Dictionary of Celtic Myth and Legend,
Thames & Hudson, 1992

Gregory, Lady Augusta
Cuchullin of Muirthemne, John Murray, 1902

Guest, Lady Charlotte
The Mabinogion (trans.), Bernard Quaritch, 1877

Guyot, Charles
La Légende de la Ville d'Ys, Coop Breizh, 1926

Johnson, W B
Folk Tales of Brittany, Methuen, 1927

Jones G & Jones T
The Mabinogion (trans.), Everyman, 1974

Joyce, P W
Old Celtic Romances, David Nutt, 1894

Kinsella, Thomas
The Tain (trans.), Oxford University Press, 1969

Laing, Lloyd
Celtic Britain, Granada, 1981

Lobineau, G-A
Les Vies des Saints de Bretagne, Méquignon Junior, 1836

McNeill, John
The Celtic Church, Cambridge University Press, 1974

Matthews, Caitlin
The Celtic Book of Days, Godsfield Press, 1995

Mitchell, John
Megalithomania, Thames & Hudson, 1982

Nash, D W
Taliesin: Bards & Druids of Britain,
John Russell Smith, 1858

Piggott, Stuart
The Druids, Thames & Hudson, 1975

Renouard, Michel
Dictionnaire de Bretagne, Ouest-France, 1992

Rich, D & Begg, E
On the Trail of Merlin, Aquarian, 1991

Sharkey, John
Celtic Mysteries, Thames & Hudson, 1975

Villemarqué, Hersart de la
Barzaz Breiz, Chants Populaires de la Bretagne, 1867

PRONUNCIATION GUIDE

The following is a general guide only and is not intended to be definitive. The suggestions below, listed in alphabetical order, will provide an accessible interpretation of character names and place-names used throughout this book.

IRELAND

Ailbine Albineh
Aillen Ahlen
Ailill Ahlil or Allyil
Athmaga Ahmoga or Awmoga
Athslisen Ahshlisen or Awshlisen
Athberena Ahberenah or Awberenah
Bodb Bove
Brúgh na Bóinne Brew neh Bone-nyeh
Conchobar Cru-hoor or Conachoor
Cruachan Krewken
Cú Chulainn Koohulann
Dechtire Deck-tir-ah
Dooros Doorus
Emain Macha Aywin Moh-ha
Emer Eemir
Ferdia Ferdiah
Fiacha Mac Conga Feeocha Mock Cungah
Fionn Fyun
Finnegas Finnegus
Gráinne Grawn-yeh
Lughnasadh Loo-neseh
Medb Mave
Muirthemne Mwir-hem-nyeh
Niamh Neeve
Oenghus (Aengus) Engus
Oisin Osheen
Saultam Sooltom
Scáthach Skawthuck
Sidhe She
Samhain Sow-in
Sliabh Culind Shleev Koolind
Slieve Fuad Shleev Foo-ad
Táin Bó Cuailnge Thawn Bow Kooling-eh

WALES

Afagddu Avathoo
Arberth Ahhbeth
Bedwyr Bedwir
Ceridwen Keridwen

Crwiwy Croo-ee
Culhwch Kulhuc
Cwm Kerwyn Coom Care-win
Cwm Cawlwyd Coom Call-wid
Dillus Varvawc Dihl-us Varv-hawc
Diwrnach Dew-r-narc
Eiddoel Eye-thoil
Geneir Gen-ay-r
Goleuddydd Goll-eye-eeth
Gwalchmai Gwalc-my
Gwalwl Gwall
Gwenhwyvar Gwen-eh-var
Gwri Goo-ree
Gwyddno Garanhir Gwith-know Gar-an-here
Hefeydd Hev-eth
Kigwri Key-goo-ree
Kilydd Kil-lith
Kyndelig Kin-delig
Morfran ab Tegid More-vran ab Tegid
Olwen All-when
Owain Oh-wine
Penllyn Pen-clin
Peredur Pear-red-ir
Plinlimmon Plin-limb-on
Pwyll Puhl
Redynvre Red-in-vire
Taliesin Tal-yesin
Tegid Voel Teg-id Voil
Teirnon Twryfliant Tie-r-non Tw-r-vliant
Twrch Trwyth Two-r-c Troo-eeth
Ysbaddaden Pencawr Us-bath-adden Pen-cow-r
Ysgeir Oervel Usgire oi-r-vel

BRITTANY

Corentin Corr-aunt-ten
Dahut Daa-hute
Efflam Ee-vlam
Gradlon Grad-lon
Guenole Jen-ole
Hyrglas Ire-glass

157

PICTURE CREDITS

Wherever possible, the Publishers have attempted to contact the copyright holders of the images reproduced in this book.

Cover: Text page from *The Book of Kells*, courtesy of the Bridgeman Art Library, London/Trinity College, Dublin; cover inset: stone cross, Mick Sharp Photography.

Page 2, The Slide File, Dublin; page 7, © British Museum, London; page 9, The National Museum of Wales; page 11, © British Museum, London; page 13, Werner Forman Archive/British Museum, London; page 15, The Slide File, Dublin; page 17, Museum of Antiquities, University and Society of Antiquaries of Newcastle upon Tyne; pages 18-19, Werner Forman Archive; page 22, AKG Photo, London (Erich Lessing)/Moravska Museum; page 25, © British Museum, London; page 26, Anthony Weir/Fortean Picture Library; page 29, Werner Forman Archive/British Museum, London; page 30, Werner Forman Archive/Musée de Rennes; page 31, © British Museum, London; page 33, left: Keltenmuseum, Hallein; right, Bernisches Historisches Museum, Bern; page 34, Werner Forman Archive/British Museum, London; page 35, Werner Forman Archive/Musée Archeologique de Breteuil; page 36, Werner Forman Archive/British Museum, London; page 38, Germanisches Nationalmuseum, Nuremberg; page 39 © Bildarchiv preussischer kulturbesitz, Berlin (photo: Kraft)/National-museum, Copenhagen; page 41, AKG Photo, London (Erich Lessing)/Rheinisches Landesmuseum, Bonn; page 43, AKG Photo, London (Erich Lessing)/Joanneum Landesmuseum, Steiermark, Graz; page 44, Werner Forman Archive/Musée des Antiquités Nationales, St Germain-en-Laye; page 45, Allen Kennedy/Fortean Picture Library; page 47, Werner Forman Archive/Natural History Museum, Vienna; page 48, Mick Sharp Photography; page 49, Musée Historique d'Orleanais, Orleans; page 51, Werner Forman Archive/British Museum, London; page 53, © Dave Longley/Mick Sharp Photottgraphy; page 54, AKG Photo, London (Erich Lessing)/National Museum, Budapest; page 55, Museum für Vor- und Frügeschite, Saarbrücken; page 56, AKG Photo, London (Erich Lessing)/Keltenmuseum, Hallein; page 57 (left) AKG Photo, London (Erich Lessing)/British Museum, London; (right) Lauros-Giraudon/Musée des Antiquités Nationales, St Germain-en-Laye; page 58, Rheinisches Landesmuseum, Trier; page 59, C M Dixon; page 61, Werner Forman Archive/The National Museum of Wales; page 62, AKG Photo, London (Erich Lessing)/Musée des Antiquités Nationales, St Germain-en-Laye; page 63, Werner Forman Archive; page 65, Lauros-Giraudon/Musée des Antiquitiés Nationales, St Germain-en-Laye; page 66, © Bildarchiv preussischer kulturbesitz, Berlin; page 67, 68, Allen Kennedy/Fortean Picture Library; page 69, C M Dixon; page 70, E.T. Archive; page 71, Musée Borely, Marseille; page 72, Werner Forman Archive/Museo Civico Romano, Brescia; page 74, National Museum of Ireland; page 75, Werner Forman Archive/British Museum, London; page 78, AKG Photo, London (Erich Lessing)/Nationalmuseum, Copenhagen; page 79, Museum of Antiquities, University and Society of Antiquaries of Newcastle upon Tyne; page 80, Werner Forman Archive/National Museum of Ireland; page 81, Rheinisches Landesmuseum, Bonn; page 83, left: Musée Bargoin, Clermont-Ferrand, right: Musée des Antiquités Nationales, St Germain-en-Laye; page 84, © British Museum, London; page 85, C M Dixon; page 87, The Bridgeman Art Library,

London/British Library, London; pages 88-9, © Jean Williamson/Mick Sharp Photography; page 92, Werner Forman Archive/National Museum, Prague; page 94, Musée Bargoin, Clermont-Ferrand; page 95, Peter Clayton/British Museum, London; page 96, Museum of London; page 97, Werner Forman Archive/Academy of Sciences, Archaeological Institute of Nitra; page 98, The National Museum of Wales; page 100, Werner Forman Archive/Náklo Museum, Olomouc; page 103, Mick Sharp Photography; page 105, Miranda Aldhouse Green/Rheinisches Landesmuseum, Bonn; page 107, The Bridgeman Art Library, London/ National Museum of Ireland; page 108, Lauros-Giraudon/Musée des Antiquités Nationales, St Germain-en-Laye; page 109, Regensburg Museum; page 112, Museum of Antiquities, University and Society of Antiquaries of Newcastle upon Tyne; page 113, Paul Broadhurst/ Fortean Picture Library; page 115, Charles Tait/Ancient Art and Architecture Collection; page 116, 117, © British Museum, London; page 118, Ancient Art and Architecture Collection; page 119, © British Museum, London; page 120, AKG Photo, London (Erich Lessing)/Manerbio, Brescia; page 121, Manx National Heritage; page 122, AKG Photo, London (Erich Lessing)/ Württemberg Landesmuseum, Stuttgart; page 125, Helga Willcocks/Sylvia Cordaiy Photo Library; page 126, © British Museum, London; page 127, Images Colour Library; pages 128-9, Werner Forman Archive; page 132, Werner Forman Archive/Slovak Museum, Martin; page 135, Werner Forman Archive/British Museum, London; page 136, © Bildarchiv preussischer kulturbesitz, Berlin; page 139, Werner Forman Archive/Dorset Natural History and Archaeology Society; page 141, Robert Estall Photo Library; page 144, AKG Photo, London (Erich Lessing)/Württemberg Landesmuseum, Stuttgart; page 145, Ancient Art and Architecture Collection; page 147, AKG Photo, London (Erich Lessing)/Rheinisches Landesmuseum, Bonn; page 150, AKG Photo, London (Erich Lessing)/National Museum, Budapest; page 152, C M Dixon; page 153, Janet and Colin Bord/Fortean Picture Library; page 154, C M Dixon; page 155, Werner Forman Archive.